Indigenous Peoples, Ethnic Groups, and the State

CULTURAL SURVIVAL STUDIES IN ETHNICITY AND CHANGE SERIES

Allyn and Bacon

David Maybury-Lewis and Theodore Macdonald, Jr., Series Editors
Cultural Survival, Inc., Harvard University

Malaysia and the "Original People": A Case Study of the Impact of Development on Indigenous Peoples by Robert Knox Dentan, Kirk Endicott, Alberto G. Gomes, and M. B. Hooker
Order No. 0-205-19817-1

Gaining Ground? Evenkis, Land, and Reform in Southeastern Siberia by Gail A. Fondahl
Order No. 0-205-27579-6

Ariaal Pastoralists of Kenya: Surviving Drought and Development in Africa's Arid Lands by Elliot Fratkin
0-205-26997-4

Ethnicity and Culture amidst New "Neighbors": The Runa of Ecuador's Amazon Region by Theodore Macdonald, Jr.
Order No. 0-205-19821-X

Indigenous Peoples, Ethnic Groups, and the State, Second Edition by David Maybury-Lewis
Order No. 0-205-33746-5

Aboriginal Reconciliation and the Dreaming: Warramiri Yolngu and the Quest for Equality by Ian S. McIntosh
Order No. 0-205-29793-5

Defending the Land: Sovereignty and Forest Life in James Bay Cree Society by Ronald Niezen
Order No. 0-205-27580-X

Forest Dwellers, Forest Protectors: Indigenous Models for International Development by Richard Reed
Order No. 0-205-19822-8

AlterNatives: Community, Identity, and Environmental Justice on Walpole Island by Robert M. VanWynsberghe
Order No. 0-205-34952-8

Second Edition

Indigenous Peoples, Ethnic Groups, and the State

David Maybury-Lewis
Harvard University

Allyn and Bacon
Boston • London • Toronto • Sydney • Tokyo • Singapore

This book is dedicated with love and gratitude
to
Anthony Maybury-Lewis and Chikako Kuno

Series Editor: Jennifer Jacobson
Series Editorial Assistant: Tom Jefferies
Marketing Manager: Judeth Hall
Cover Designer: Joel Gendron
Editorial-Production Service: Omegatype Typography, Inc.
Electronic Composition: Omegatype Typography, Inc.

ISBN: 0-205-33746-5

Printed in the United States of America

10 9 8 7 6   06   05   04

Maps on pages xiii, xiv, and inside the back cover provided by Carl Mehler,
National Geographic Books.

Contents

Foreword to the Series

Cultural Survival is an organization founded in 1972 to defend the human rights of indigenous peoples, who are those, like the Indians of the Americas, who have been dominated and marginalized by peoples different from themselves. Since the states that claim jurisdiction over indigenous peoples consider them aliens and inferiors, they are among the world's most underprivileged minorities, facing a constant threat of physical extermination and cultural annihilation. This is no small matter, for indigenous peoples make up approximately five percent of the world's population. Most of them wish to become successful ethnic minorities, meaning that they be permitted to maintain their own traditions even though they are out of the mainstream in the countries where they live. Indigenous peoples hope therefore for multiethnic states that will tolerate diversity in their midst. In this their cause is the cause of ethnic minorities worldwide and is one of the major issues of our times, for the vast majority of states in the world are multi-ethnic. The question is whether states are willing to accept and live peaceably with ethnic differences, or whether they will treat them as an endless source of conflict.

Cultural Survival works to promote multi-ethnic solutions to otherwise conflictive situations. It sponsors research, advocacy and publications which examine situations of ethnic conflict, especially (but not exclusively) as they affect indigenous peoples, and suggests solutions for them. It also provides technical and legal assistance to indigenous peoples and organizations.

This series of monographs entitled "Cultural Survival Studies in Ethnicity and Change Series" is published in collaboration with Allyn and Bacon (the Pearson Education Group). It will focus on problems of ethnicity in the modern world and how they affect the interrelations between indigenous peoples, ethnic groups and the state.

The studies will focus on the situations of ethnic minorities and of indigenous peoples, who are a special kind of ethnic minority, as they try to defend their rights, their resources and their ways of life within modern states. Some of the volumes in the series will deal with general themes, such as ethnic conflict, indigenous rights, socioeconomic development or multiculturalism. These volumes will contain brief case studies to illustrate their general arguments. Meanwhile, the series as a whole plans to publish a larger number of books that deal in depth with specific cases. It is our conviction that good case studies are essential for a better understanding of issues that arouse such passion in the world today, and this series will provide them. Its emphasis nevertheless will be on relating the particular to the general in the comparative contexts of national or international affairs.

The books in the series will be short, averaging 100 to 150 pages in length, and written in a clear and accessible style aimed at students and the general reader. They are intended to clarify issues that are often obscure or misunderstood and that are not treated succinctly elsewhere. It is our hope, therefore, that they will also prove useful as reference works for scholars, activists and policy makers.

David Maybury-Lewis
Theodore Macdonald, Jr.
Cultural Survival, Inc.
215 Prospect Street
Cambridge, MA 02139
(617) 441-5400 fax: (617) 441-5417

Preface

This is the first in a series of monographs on ethnicity and social change sponsored by Cultural Survival. Our organization has worked to defend the human rights of indigenous peoples since its founding in 1972. Our publications, particularly the *Cultural Survival Quarterly,* are being used by schools and universities in many countries. This new series is intended to supply the need for concise studies of issues and cases related to problems of ethnicity, marginal peoples, ethnic minorities, and states that are trying either to suppress or to accommodate the minorities in their populations. The books are written for students and the general reader. It is our hope that they will clarify issues that are often obscure and that are normally only dealt with in learned journals, and that they will in this way prove valuable as reference tools that specialists and policy makers may also find useful.

Ethnicity is one of the obscurest issues of them all. In spite of the fact that there is much talk nowadays about ethnicity and ethnic groups, it is not always clear exactly what that means or why ethnicity should have such a powerful hold on human imagination and behavior. Ethnic conflict has supplanted communism as the specter that is haunting the world. Writers, commentators, and newspapers are currently telling us that people everywhere are giving in to the primordial urge to band together with others like themselves and to harass or kill those who are different.

In this book I argue that they are wrong. A closer look at ethnicity shows that it is not an innate attribute of human beings, but rather a potential that all of us have and that may or may not be activated. Nor do feelings of ethnic solidarity inevitably lead to conflict when they are activated. It all depends on the context. I therefore look closely at the history and politics of interethnic situations and at the agendas of those leaders who incite their followers to enter into conflict with peoples of other ethnic groups.

Ideally, these central issues should be examined much more thoroughly than I am able to within the limitations of a short monograph. In particular, I would have liked to go into more detail on the views of their own past that inform the ideologies of ethnic groups and the differing visions of history that separate them from each other. History is, after all, a matter of making sense of and trying to give meaning to the past. More often than not, conflict between ethnic groups involves contested meanings. In this book I do not have the space to analyze the contesting views of history held by parties to ethnic conflicts. Had I attempted to do so, I would have been forced to sacrifice the comparisons presented here. These more intimate analyses of ideology and history will be found in the other books in this series, which present more detailed studies of particular cases.

Another issue that is much misunderstood concerns indigenous peoples. There is a great deal of confusion about exactly who they are, where they are, and what their place should be in the modern world. It is not often realized that they make up some 5 percent of the world's population; that they are not marginal peoples who are disappearing but rather marginalized peoples who are seeking accommodation with the states in which they live. They are a special case of ethnic minorities. In fact it is often hard to determine whether a society should be classified as an indigenous or an ethnic minority because there is no hard and fast distinction between these categories. We deal instead with a continuum of minorities. Indigenous peoples are normally the smallest in numbers and the most alien to the mainstream of the states in which they live. They are, in some places, indistinguishable from ethnic groups that, in turn, are often considered to be nations, although they do not control states.

I discuss the special circumstances of these different gradations of minorities, always with reference to the state that has to decide whether to recognize their distinctiveness; if so, how to accommodate it and, if not, how to suppress it. In the final chapter I suggest that both theorists and rulers of the state have traditionally preferred to think and act as if the populations of states were already homogenous or soon would be. I then discuss the growing realization that most states in the world are multiethnic, and consider the difficulties of making such states work smoothly and without too much conflict. Finally I suggest that these difficulties are not much greater than those we confront when we try to make democracies work in a similar fashion.

Acknowledgments

I want to thank my colleagues and collaborators in Cultural Survival who have pointed out the need for a discussion of the issues involving indigenous peoples, ethnicity, and the state and urged me to try my hand at it. I am especially grateful to those who wrote for the *Cultural Survival Quarterly* on these issues and whose works, as may be seen from my references, I have relied on heavily to present the case studies and specific details that appear in this book. The book was written during the term of a Jennings Randolph Fellowship at the United States Institute of Peace in Washington. I am enormously grateful to the Institute for providing me, at least, with enough peace to write and enough discussion to make the writing a less lonely experience than it might have been. In this connection I especially want to thank my fellow Fellows, who were not only good company but were always amiably willing to discuss ideas and make suggestions as well. Joe Klaits and Sally Blair of the Jennings Randolph Program saw to it that I had everything I needed to get on with my work and Frederick Williams and Kerry O'Donnell extricated me with unfailing good humor from potential computer disasters. I am most grateful to them all. I also want to thank Nicole Thornton-Burnett for looking after my affairs at Harvard while I was away and keeping me supplied with references and information from home whenever I needed them. Meanwhile in Washington I was propped up by Denis McDonough. I am deeply grateful for his imaginative and efficient assistance, without which I could never have completed this book during the period of my Fellowship. Finally, I want to thank my wife Pia and my son Biorn for encouraging me to write this book and arguing with me creatively during the writing of it.

I would like to thank the United States Institute of Peace for awarding me a second half-year Jennings Randolph Fellowship. I was especially pleased that the first task completed during this Fellowship was to submit the revised copy of this book for its second edition. I want to thank as well the people who worked so hard and so creatively to send the second edition to press. Urfa Qadri proofread the entire volume and suggested corrections and emendations for the second edition. Linda Ordogh was as knowledgeable and helpful as always, as she supplied me with references and information from my home base in Cambridge. Heather Staley organized the second edition with a combination of good humor and attention to detail that I found both admirable and refreshing. I am deeply grateful to them all. Finally, I would like to thank the following reviewers: Catherine Cutbill, Ramapo College of New Jersey; Christina Kreps, University of Denver; Christine A. Loveland, Shippensburg University; and Phyllis Morrow, University of Alaska Fairbanks.

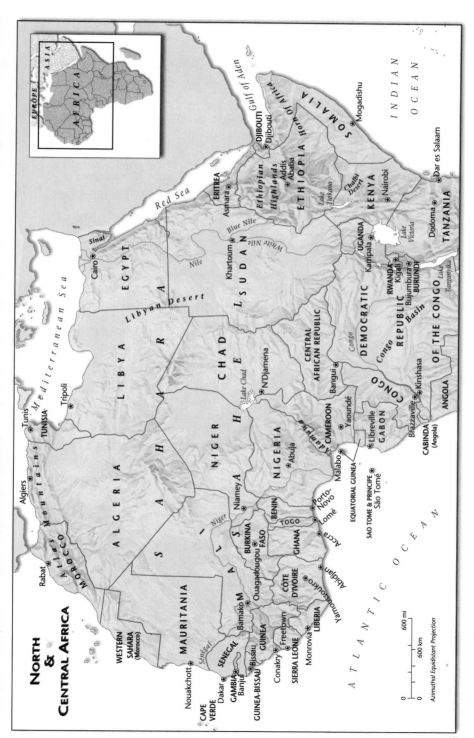

NORTH & CENTRAL AFRICA

EUROPE ASIA
AFRICA

Mediterranean Sea

Algiers
Tunis
TUNISIA
Tripoli

MOROCCO
Rabat
Atlas Mountains

ALGERIA

LIBYA

S A H A R A

Cairo
Sinai
E G Y P T

Red Sea

Libyan Desert

Gulf of Aden

DJIBOUTI
Djibouti

ERITREA
Asmara

Ethiopian
Highlands
Addis
Ababa

E T H I O P I A *Horn of Africa*

SOMALIA
Mogadishu

INDIAN
OCEAN

Blue Nile
Khartoum
White Nile
S U D A N
Nile

Chalbi
Desert
Lake
Turkana

KENYA
Nairobi
Dar es Salaam

N I G E R
Niamey

CHAD
N'Djamena
Lake Chad

CENTRAL
AFRICAN REPUBLIC
Bangui

UGANDA
Kampala
Lake
Victoria

RWANDA
Kigali
Bujumbura
BURUNDI

Congo
DEMOCRATIC
REPUBLIC
OF THE CONGO
Congo Basin

Lake
Tanganyika

TANZANIA
Dodoma

Kinshasa

ANGOLA

MAURITANIA
Nouakchott

MALI

Bamako

Niger

S A H E L

BURKINA
FASO
Ouagadougou

NIGERIA
Abuja

Adamawa

CAMEROON
Yaoundé

Malabo

EQUATORIAL GUINEA

Libreville
GABON

Brazzaville
CONGO

CABINDA
(Angola)

SAO TOME & PRINCIPE
São Tomé

BENIN
Porto-
Novo
TOGO
Lomé

GHANA
Accra

CÔTE
D'IVOIRE
Yamoussoukro
Abidjan

CAPE
VERDE

Dakar
SENEGAL
Banjul
GAMBIA
Bissau
GUINEA-BISSAU
GUINEA
Conakry
Freetown
SIERRA LEONE
Monrovia
LIBERIA

WESTERN
SAHARA
(Morocco)

Senegal

A T L A N T I C   O C E A N

600 mi
600 km
0

Azimuthal Equidistant Projection

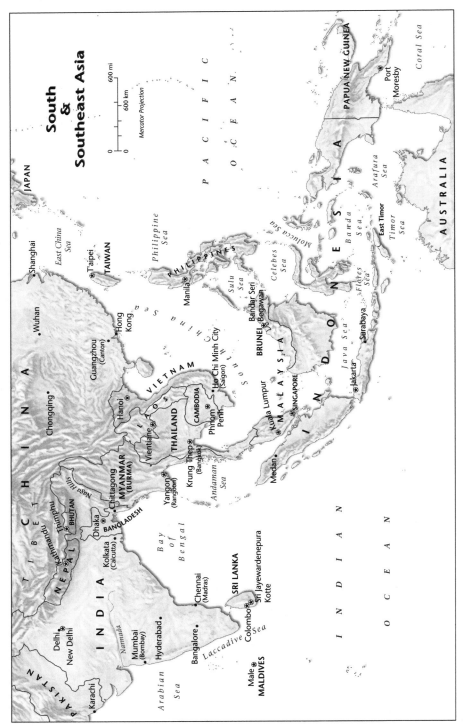

South
&
Southeast Asia

600 mi

600 km

Mercator Projection

PACIFIC OCEAN

Coral Sea

JAPAN

East China Sea

Shanghai

Wuhan

Taipei
TAIWAN

Hong Kong

Guangzhou
(Canton)

Chongqing

C H I N A

T I B E T

PAKISTAN

Karachi

Delhi
New Delhi

Mumbai
(Bombay)

Hyderabad

Bangalore

I N D I A

Narmada

Arabian
Sea

Laccadive
Sea

Male
MALDIVES

NEPAL

Kathmandu

Thimphu

BHUTAN

Naga Hills

Chittagong

MYANMAR
(BURMA)

Yangon
(Rangoon)

Dhaka

BANGLADESH

Kolkata
(Calcutta)

Bay
of
Bengal

Chennai
(Madras)

SRI LANKA

Colombo

Sri Jayewardenepura
Kotte

I N D I A N   O C E A N

Hanoi

V I E T N A M

L A O S

Vientiane

THAILAND

Krung Thep
(Bangkok)

Andaman
Sea

CAMBODIA

Phnom
Penh

Ho Chi Minh City
(Saigon)

South China Sea

Philippine
Sea

PHILIPPINES

Manila

Sulu
Sea

Celebes
Sea

Molucca Sea

BRUNEI

Bandar Seri
Begawan

Medan

M A L A Y S I A

Kuala Lumpur

SINGAPORE

I N D O N E S I A

Jakarta

Java Sea

Surabaya

Flores
Sea

Borda
Sea

Banda
Sea

Arafura
Sea

East Timor

Timor
Sea

PAPUA NEW GUINEA

Port
Moresby

AUSTRALIA

xiv

Indigenous Peoples

GENOCIDE IN THE AMERICAS

Indigenous peoples have all too often been the victims of genocide. As Charles Darwin noted "Wherever the European has trod, death seems to pursue the aboriginal" (Merivale 1842: 204). Nowhere is this more true than in the Americas, whose native inhabitants have been intermittently slaughtered by invaders and their descendents since the conquest. In fact the demographic consequences of that invasion are the most drastic that the world has ever known. They were heightened by the unique circumstances of the encounter, which was the most extraordinary meeting in the history of humankind. It brought together two large portions of the human race that had virtually lost touch with each other and been separated for at least forty thousand years.

Eduardo Galeano, a distinguished Uruguayan writer, captures the surreal quality of that encounter in a brilliant description at the beginning of his quartet entitled *Memories of Fire:*

> He falls on his knees, weeps, kisses the earth. He steps forward, staggering because for more than a month he has hardly slept, and beheads some shrubs with his sword.

> Then he raises the flag. On one knee, eyes lifted to heaven, he pronounces three times the names of Isabella and Ferdinand. Beside him the scribe, Rodrigo de Escobedo, a man slow of pen, draws up the document.

> From today everything belongs to those remote monarchs: the coral sea, the beaches, the rocks all green with moss, the woods, the parrots, and these laurel-skinned people who don't yet know about clothes, sin, or money and gaze dazedly at the scene.

Luis de Torres translates Christopher Columbus' questions into Hebrew: "Do you know the kingdom of the Great Khan? Where does the gold you have in your noses and ears come from?"

The naked men stare at him with open mouths, and the interpreter tries out his small stock of Chaldean: "Gold? Temples? Palaces? King of Kings? Gold?"

Then he tries his Arabic, the little he knows of it: "Japan? China? Gold?"

The interpreter apologizes to Columbus in the language of Castile.

Columbus curses in Genovese and throws to the ground his credentials, written in Latin and addressed to the Great Khan. The naked men watch the anger of the intruder with red hair and coarse skin, who wears a velvet cape and very shiny clothes. (1985: 45–46)

A century later the indigenous population of the entire hemisphere had been cut in half. Initially they were massacred. Later they were worked to death in the mines or on the plantations. But the greatest killer was disease and the famine and dislocation that went with it. Native Americans had no immunity from the diseases that the Europeans brought with them and whole populations succumbed to pestilence. With so many people dying and the invaders making such demands on the labor of those who survived, there were in many parts of the Americas not enough people to tend to the crops, so that famine also ravaged the indigenous populations. The sense of death and despair engendered by this terrible history is well summed up in the words of a Maya chronicler who wrote:

Before…they (the Indians) had no sickness; they had no aching bones; they had no burning chest; they had no abdominal pain; they had no consumption; they had no headache. At that time the course of humanity was orderly. The foreigners made it otherwise when they arrived here…. Let us therefore die! Let us therefore perish! For our Gods are already dead!

What happened to the native peoples of the Americas is, on a vast scale, that which has been happening and continues to happen to indigenous peoples the world over. The history of the Americas is also revealing in another way, for it shows very clearly the circumstances under which the massacre of indigenous peoples is carried out and the circumstances under which other policies are usually adopted.

In countries with sparse indigenous populations, such as the United States, Brazil, or Argentina, Indians were not traditionally thought to have any place within the nation. In colonial Brazil the Portuguese *bandeirantes* became famous as tough explorers of the back-lands, so much so that they occupy the same mythical position in Brazilian culture and in Brazilian schoolbooks as the pioneers do in the United States. What the schoolbooks gloss over is that the *bandeirantes* were ruthless and expert slavers, who specialized in penetrating deep into the forests and attacking Indian villages that thought they were remote enough to be safe. The *bandeirantes* were so efficient that they succeeded in depopulating large swaths of Brazil. In any case, the indigenous populations were too small to supply the labor required by the sugar plantations that soon provided the wealth of colonial Brazil, so they were replaced by black slaves brought in from Africa. After that in Brazil, just as in the United States and Argentina, the Indians were thought of as peoples beyond the frontier, inhabiting "Indian territory," a national region that was steadily eroded until each country swallowed it up in the name of its own national destiny.

Argentina had its own southward push in the nineteenth century, similar to the westward push in the United States. It was launched by General Roca's famous campaign in 1879–80, known in Argentina as the Conquest of the Desert, which was expressly intended to annihilate the Indians of the pampas and to seize and redistribute their lands and their large herds of cattle. Roca justified his genocidal strategy when he wrote: "Our self respect as a virile people obliges us to put down this handful of savages as soon as possible either by reason or by force, for they destroy our principle wealth and prevent us from occupying, definitively and in the name of law, progress and our own security the richest and most fertile lands of the Republic" (Serres Güiraldes 1979: 377–8).

Teddy Roosevelt expressed similar sentiments when he wrote in *The Winning of the West:* "The settler and pioneer have at bottom had justice on their side; this great continent could not have been kept as nothing but a game preserve for squalid savages" (Roosevelt 1889: 90).

The Brazilian push to the west came a century later, in the 1960s, and it was no coincidence that it had such harsh effects on the remote indigenous peoples who were overtaken by it and Brazil was later accused of genocide. There is no evidence that the Brazilian government planned to massacre Indians as it encouraged the "opening up" of the backlands, but there is plenty of evidence that Brazilian frontiersmen did. Meanwhile the government encouraged "development" by whatever means and did little to protect the indigenous peoples who were predictably killed or dispossessed in the process.[1]

---

1. This genocidal process still continues. See the section on the Yanomami Indians on pp. 20–23.

The killing of indigenous people is usually resorted to when outsiders wish to seize the lands and resources they control or when indigenous populations are simply considered to be "in the way" of national destiny, development, resource extraction, dam building, or anything else. Genocide is, for obvious reasons, not the policy of choice where outsiders need their labor, although there are exceptions to this. The most notorious exception in the Americas is the treatment bordering on genocide of the rubber tappers in the Amazon region.

Unfortunately for the indigenous peoples of the region, rubber trees grow wild throughout the Amazon basin. When the development of rubber tires in the nineteenth century sent the price of wild rubber soaring, it set off a rubber frenzy in large areas of Brazil, Colombia, Peru, and Bolivia. Fortunes could be and were made by those who controlled the collection and marketing of rubber, but for this they needed a docile labor force. Rubber gatherers had to walk through the forests, tapping the trees along their route and then bringing the latex back to a collection point, a highly labor intensive operation. Rubber collectors were thus faced with the problem of acquiring a large labor force and preventing their wandering laborers from running away if they did not like their conditions of work. They solved it by seizing whole communities of indigenous peoples, forcing some of them to gather rubber and holding the others hostage to guarantee the tappers' return. This control, never lenient, degenerated in some areas to a level of sadism that is horrifying to contemplate. A traveller along the Ucayali river in the Peruvian Amazon wrote in 1874 that "On these rivers all is fright, shock, dread and panic-terror; no one on them thinks himself secure and not even life is guaranteed here" (Brown and Fernández 1991: 99). The notorious Peruvian, Julio Arana, set himself up with British capital on the Putumayo river (which now forms the boundary between Peru and Colombia). There he and his henchmen killed, tortured, raped, and otherwise mistreated his indigenous captives as much for amusement as to instill in them the terror necessary for the extraction of the last ounce of rubber. The horrors along the Putumayo were finally exposed by a courageous Peruvian. They were investigated and publicized by Roger Casement, a British consular official who provoked a parliamentary investigation in London of what was being done with British capital and by British subjects (many of Arana's overseers were imported from Barbados) in the wilds of Peru. Arana was too influential a man to be punished however; besides, the Peruvian government was not unhappy to support his brand of "development" in the wilds, especially when the developers safeguarded the nation's frontier by chasing away the Colombians in the region. So Arana lived out his days in the Amazonian town of Iquitos. The Amazonian rubber boom and the related sufferings of the Amazonian Indians were eventually brought to an end by the British, but for commercial rather than humanitarian reasons. An Englishman succeeded in smuggling rubber seedlings out of Brazil. These were carefully tended at Kew Gardens in London and then sent out to be replanted in southeast Asia. By the 1920s rubber could be produced more cheaply and in larger quantities in the plantations of southeast Asia than by the collectors in the South American jungles, so the Amazonian rubber industry collapsed.

The massacre of indigenous peoples during the rubber boom is an extreme case, for it risked destroying the very labor force on which the wealth of the collectors depended. One can only surmise that Arana and his henchmen wished to control their indigenous workers through sheer terror, and that eventually they created a regime in which cruelty was piled on cruelty, simply because there was no one to stop it (see Taussig 1986). Much more common throughout the Americas, in areas where there is a substantial indigenous population whose labor is needed by its overlords, have been policies designed to force the Indians to do the work required of them. Even after the colonial policies of slavery and forced labor had been abolished, other mechanisms were put in place to accomplish the same ends. Indian lands were systematically taken away from their owners, who became a source of cheap labor once they were living in poverty on reduced holdings. Strenuous efforts were made to destroy indigenous communities by forcing them to divide up their common lands and hold them in individual parcels. Systems of debt peonage were institutionalized, especially in the Andean countries, under which Indians were tricked or forced into accepting contracts that they did not understand and often tried unsuccessfully to repudiate—contracts that required them to work for long periods of time for miserable wages or for payment in kind. Alternatively laws were passed, as in Guatemala and El Salvador, requiring indigenous peoples to work a certain number of days each year for private employers and to carry pass books to show that they were doing so. If all this was not enough, Indians were simply required to perform certain kinds of forced labor. Unpaid work on the roads was, for example, compulsory for all Indians in Peru well into this century.

The Americas furnish the oldest and most dramatic example of the treatment of indigenous peoples. It was the invasion of the Americas that marked the beginning of European expansion and it is the Indians of the Americas who have borne the brunt of their indigenous status for the longest time; but similar processes have taken place all over the world.

INDIGENOUS PEOPLES: SUBORDINATED AND MARGINALIZED

When the Spanish landed in the Americas they referred to all the natives of the New World as *Indians*, following Columbus's famous confusion. It was clear, though, that the Indians were indigenous to the Americas and the Europeans were not. It was some time later that people of European descent, but born in the Americas, started to think of themselves as "indigenous" to the Americas too. Nevertheless, Indians or Native Americans are to this day still considered the truly indigenous Americans as opposed to others born in the Americas whose ancestors, however distant, came from overseas.

This ambiguity is not peculiar to the Americas. The very term *indigenous peoples* is confusing because most people in the world are "indigenous" to their countries in the sense of having been born in them or being descended from people who were born in them. Indigenous peoples are clearly native to their countries in this sense too, but they also make another claim, namely that they were there first and are still there and so have rights of prior occupancy to their lands. This criterion discriminates clearly enough between, for example, Native Americans and all those who came to the Americas after Columbus's invasion. It also distinguishes well enough between indigenous peoples and later comers in other parts of the world that have been colonized from overseas. There is no problem in distinguishing the Aborigines of Australia or the Maoris of New Zealand as "indigenous" in contrast to the settlers who came later to those lands; but such distinctions are not so easy to draw in Europe or Asia or Africa. In those continents, peoples have eddied this way and that, often for thousands of years, leaving in place a mosaic of different peoples who dispute the land and sometimes dispute the claim to prior occupancy of it. There are therefore additional criteria that must be used to define indigenous peoples for the purposes of any general discussion.

Indigenous peoples claim their lands because they were there first or have occupied them since time immemorial. They are also groups that have been conquered by peoples racially, ethnically, or culturally different from themselves. They have thus been subordinated by or incorporated in alien states that treat them as outsiders and, usually, as inferiors. Isolated or marginal groups that have not yet been conquered by a state are also considered indigenous, because it is only a matter of time before they are subordinated. Indigenous peoples maintain their own languages, which normally differ from those spoken by the mainstream populations, and their own cultures, which invariably differ from the mainstream. They are conscious of their separate identities and normally struggle to retain these. The salient characteristic of indigenous peoples, then, is that they are marginal to or dominated by the states that claim jurisdiction over them.

Since they had not developed their own states and are not integral to the states that now actually or potentially rule over them, indigenous peoples are often referred to as *tribal*. The phrase *tribal peoples* is unfortunately imprecise, but it is often used nowadays as a kind of shorthand to refer to small-scale, preindustrial societies that live in comparative isolation and manage their affairs without any centralized authority such as the state. The worldwide tendency is for such peoples sooner or later to be conquered by states. Since the states then consider them aliens and inferiors, indigenous or tribal peoples are among the world's most underprivileged minorities, facing the constant threat of genocide or ethnocide.

Genocide (the physical extermination of a defined category of people) is today universally condemned. In fact, one of the first acts of the newly created United Nations, acting in response to the horrors perpetrated by the Nazis during World War II, was to approve a Convention on Genocide in 1948. The problem, as we shall see in Chapter 3, is that genocide is extremely difficult either to prevent or to punish. It requires international action against the perpetrators and that is very rarely possible to organize. Genocide, therefore, continues to take place and indigenous peoples are especially at risk because they are so vulnerable.

Ethnocide (the destruction of a people's way of life) is, on the other hand, often not even condemned when it comes to indigenous peoples. On the contrary, it is advocated as an appropriate policy toward them. Indigenous peoples are normally looked down on as "backward," so it is presumed that their ways of life must be destroyed, partly in order to civilize them and partly to enable them to coexist with others in the modern world.

A people's way of life is often referred to by social scientists as its *culture*, a term that indicates the totality of ideas, attitudes, customs, and ways of doing things that people acquire as members of a society. Often the institutions of a society are also considered part of its culture, although some scholars prefer to make a distinction between *culture*, which is largely ideational, and *social structure*, which refers to the institutional arrangements made by people who share a given culture. In this book the term *culture* is used to refer generally to the distinctive way of life of a given people. It is the cultures of indigenous peoples that are regularly threatened, even when their lives are not at risk, and it is to their cultures that they often cling in order to give meaning and dignity to their lives.

As we shall see, there is no hard and fast distinction between indigenous peoples and other kinds of localized ethnic groups. Who then are the peoples generally considered "indigenous" and how many of them are there? The second question is even harder to answer than the first one for it obviously depends on who is considered indigenous (see Table 1.1). Even in the Americas, where the indigenous category is relatively easy to define, indigenous peoples are very hard to count. In places where it is a stigma to be considered "Indian," people will be reluctant to admit to it and will claim that they are of mixed blood or that they are participants in the mainstream national culture. Recently, as the indigenous rights movement has gathered steam internationally, people who once claimed not to be Indian now claim that they in fact are. There may also be political considerations that influence the over- or undercounting of Indians. At certain times in the history of the Americas, individual countries have decided that Indianness was a stigma that should be abolished in the name of egalitarianism and democracy. They have therefore

TABLE 1.1 WORLD INDIGENOUS POPULATION BY REGION OF THE WORLD

Region	Population
Canada	935,000
United States	1,783,600
Central America and Mexico	12,713,000
South America	16,000,000
Greenland	58,000
Total of the Americas	31,489,600
China	91,000,000
Philippines	6,500,000
South Asia	60,000,000
Southeast Asia	20,000,000
Japan/Pacific Islands	750,000
Total Asia	178,250,000
Australia	250,000
New Zealand	325,000
Scandinavia	58,000
Former Soviet Union	28,000,000
Africa	14,200,000
Arabia	5,000,000
Total World Indigenous Populations	257,572,600

abolished the category of "Indian" altogether and proclaimed that there were no more Indians in the nation. A reasonable guess as to the indigenous population of the Americas at the end of the twentieth century would put it at about 31.5 million, with something less than a million in Canada, about 1.75 million in the United States, somewhat less than 13 million in Mexico and Central America, and about 16 million in South America. In addition, there are about fifty-eight thousand Inuit (Eskimo) in Greenland.

In other parts of the world even the category of "indigenous" is difficult to define, let alone determine how many people belong to it. The best we can do is to give rough estimates of how many people are thought to belong in the categories that are locally considered indigenous or equivalent to indigenous. The major indigenous group in Europe are the Sami (previously known as the Lapps) who inhabit the far northern reaches of Norway, Sweden, Finland, and Russia and number about fifty-eight thousand. There are about 28 million indigenous people in the former Soviet Union and perhaps 5 million more in Arabia and the Near East. China has 91 million people classified as belonging to national minorities (see Chapter 2). Indigenous people are also found in South Asia (about 60 million), Southeast Asia and Indonesia (about 20 million), and the Philippines (about 6.5 million). Japan contains one sizeable indigenous group, the Ainu of the far north. These, together with the indigenous peoples of the Pacific islands, total perhaps seven hundred fifty thousand. The Aborigines of Australia (about a quarter of a million) and the Maoris of New Zealand (over three hundred thousand) are also clearly indigenous. In Africa it is particularly difficult to distinguish between indigenous peoples and other ethnic minorities, but I have here included in the indigenous category some African peoples who are conventionally considered to be tribal outsiders in their own countries, such as the San and related peoples (Bushmen) of the Kalahari desert, the Efe and related peoples (Pygmies) of the Ituri rainforest in Zaïre, and the nomads who roam the Sahara or who follow their herds in East Africa, all of whom add up to something over 14 million.

It will be seen that indigenous peoples, though they are difficult to define or to count and though they are largely ignored by the world, in fact make up about 5 percent of the total population of the globe. They are the descendants of peoples who were marginalized by the major powers and especially the expanding empires in their regions of the world—the European overseas empires in the Americas, Africa, Asia and Australasia, and the Russian and Chinese land empires in the heartland of Eurasia.

The expansion of these empires routinely led to the mistreatment of indigenous peoples. This is not the place to go into detail about the drastic consequences of colonial rule[2] for indigenous societies. Some examples establish the main line of my argument. The demographic consequences were disastrous everywhere. Indigenous peoples were conquered by superior weaponry. Sometimes they were subject to campaigns of extermination. More often they were driven off their lands or confined to a portion of them, if they did not flee. Meanwhile they were highly susceptible to infections transmitted by their more cosmopolitan conquerors. The results were impoverishment, starvation, and disease, which also took a fearful toll on their populations. It is difficult to calculate the exact extent of this indigenous depopulation, but Bodley combed the most reliable sources and came to the startling conclusion that indigenous peoples in the Americas, Oceania, and Africa lost about 90 percent of their population between the time of first contact and the lowest population levels experienced in the nineteenth century (1975: 39).

These figures are easier to believe if we remember the circumstances and, above all, the attitudes that accompanied the imperial conquests. Australia under the British was considered in law to be *terra nullius,* a no man's land, technically uninhabited, in which settlers on occasion hunted Aborigines for sport as if they were game animals. The original inhabitants of Tasmania were systematically exterminated. When the authorities grew tired of their "attacks on the settlers," they arranged for a line of armed men to advance across the island, again like beaters in a hunt, to flush out the remaining natives, so that they could be shot down. When the Belgians administered the Congo, atrocities were committed against native peoples that paralleled those of the Peruvian Putumayo and exceeded them in scale. It was the events in the Congo that inspired Joseph Conrad's novel *The Heart of Darkness.* It was also in the Congo that Roger Casement had his first experience of investigating horror, before he was sent across the world to look into the brutalities on the Putumayo. The Germans in Southwest Africa ordered the Herero off their grazing lands and into the desert, where they would certainly have starved. When the Herero refused, the German army carried out a war of extermination against them.

Darwin's comment about death following in the footsteps of the European told a bitter truth, but it was not the whole truth. The imperialist expansion that changed the face of the globe in the centuries since Columbus's invasion of the Americas was largely, but not entirely, a European affair. When, for example, the Japanese began to

---

2. Which, of course, includes the continuing rule of American countries over their indigenous inhabitants.

take colonies, the marginal, indigenous people in them were treated in much the same way as they were in European-ruled territories. Furthermore, countries that have not known European colonial rule, such as China, or that have thrown it off, like India, Indonesia, and various nations of Africa, still practice a kind of internal colonialism toward their own marginal populations.

IMPERIALISM AND EVOLUTIONARY THEORY

The nineteenth-century racism of Europeans and their descendants in the Americas was peculiarly virulent because it was buttressed by the theories of evolution and social Darwinism, which seemed to provide scientific support for what otherwise might have been recognized as naked prejudice. It had not always been so. From the earliest days of the European expansion into the Americas, the justification of conquest and imperialism had been much discussed. In fact, the issues were formally debated before King Charles V of Spain and a council of fourteen leading theologians who were summoned to Valladolid in 1550 to hear Bartolomé de las Casas argue the case for indigenous rights against Juan de Sepúlveda. Sepúlveda invoked Aristotle's doctrine of "natural slavery" to argue that some peoples are naturally inferior to others, who therefore have a right to enslave them and to make war on them, should they refuse to submit. Las Casas replied with a massive rebuttal of Aristotle's thesis and arguments to the effect that Spanish condemnation of indigenous customs was ill-informed, prejudiced, and, as we would now say, ethnocentric.[3] Las Casas was not alone in taking such a tolerant and enlightened view. Jean de Léry, a French Calvinist pastor, wrote a sympathetic account of the Tupinambá Indians in his *History of a Voyage to the Land of Brazil* (1578). His tolerance for Tupinambá custom was all the more remarkable because the Tupinambá, who were redoubtable warriors, did practice ritual cannibalism. This horrified the Europeans, even though they themselves routinely used judicial torture and practiced unspeakable cruelties on each other at the time (and had even been known to kill and eat each other in the religious wars that were then raging). Jean de Léry concluded that the conditions of life for the Tupinambá were somewhat better than they were for ordinary people in France. Later writers such as Montaigne and Rousseau displayed a similar rational tolerance toward the customs of exotic peoples. When such ideas carried the day and were reflected in the opinions

---

3. This historic debate is well described in Hanke 1959.

and the laws of kings, they always encountered opposition at the frontier but even this tension, which could on occasion be protective of indigenous rights, evaporated in the nineteenth century.

In the nineteenth century, learned opinion increasingly came to be scientific opinion, and scientific theory seemed at last to have resolved the question of the status of indigenous peoples. This was made possible by the new data that had become available. As the European powers consolidated their empires over most of the globe, they gathered enormous amounts of information about the distant peoples of the earth. Better still, this information could be ordered in terms of a theory that would enable western scholars to analyze the whole march of human history on scientific principles. This theory (or rather these theories, for there were innumerable variants of it) was a theory of social evolution, modeled on Darwin's theory of the evolution of the species and claiming to do for the social development of humankind what Darwin's theory had done for its physical development. A spate of books followed Darwin's *On the Origin of the Species*, all claiming to elucidate human history in a scientific and evolutionary framework. All of them placed tribal societies and indigenous peoples at or close to the bottom of the ladder of development. The writers' own societies (often simply glossed as "civilization") were invariably found at the top. Europeans and their descendants tended in any case to think that it was in the natural order of things for stronger and more "advanced" peoples to conquer and rule over weaker and more "backward" ones—a variation on Aristotle's argument cited earlier. Now they felt they had the scientific evidence that proved their superiority and justified their imperialism. The reasoned tolerance that had sometimes characterized the thinking of earlier scholars, as they tried to understand societies very different from their own, gave way in the nineteenth century to evolutionary disdain.

Once it was accepted as scientific truth that colonists and settlers represented societies that were on higher rungs of the evolutionary ladder than the savages they confronted, then this provided moral justification for almost anything that the former might do to the latter. If the settlers and the pioneers "had justice on their side," as Teddy Roosevelt insisted, then they need have no qualms about dispossessing the Indians. If the Indians were in any case no better than "squalid savages," as Teddy Roosevelt also said, then it followed that they could be severely treated by the bearers of civilization who came to take their lands and, if necessary, their lives. Such attitudes naturally bred others that were summed up in General Sheridan's notorious comment that "The only good Indian is a dead Indian."

The attitudes of nineteenth-century racism and evolutionism are no longer unquestioningly accepted throughout the world, but a certain neo-evolutionism has taken their place. Indigenous (or tribal) societies are rarely called "savage" these days, at least not in public, but they are normally considered "backward." It may no longer be considered acceptable to remove them by massacring them (though this still happens), but it is everywhere the case that governments feel that such peoples should be helped or forced to overcome their "backwardness." To overcome its backwardness, an indigenous society is urged to abandon its traditional way of life and often its language as well, usually in the hope that in so doing it will cease to exist as a society altogether. Its individual members, now no longer embedded in their backward society, will disappear into the population of the rest of the country.

ETHNOCIDE AND ITS JUSTIFICATIONS

Mexico

Two examples from the Americas show the complex reasoning that leads governments to seek to abolish indigenous cultures, and these will introduce a discussion of ethnocide as a worldwide phenomenon.

Mexico is a country with a strong official ideology that it is a mestizo nation, created out of the racial mixture of Whites and Indians and the blending of their respective cultures. Yet its elites have worried for a long time over the backwardness of the nation's large Indian population. Even former President Benito Juárez, the founder of modern Mexico and himself part Indian and proud of it, shared this concern. So his reform laws (issued in 1856) were intended to modernize Mexican agriculture and Mexican society. They would modernize agriculture by breaking up the vast holdings of the Church and other major landowners. It was hoped that this would create a proper market in land, encourage more productive smallholders, and provide lands for the many of the landless. In order to accomplish this, the communal landholdings that indigenous communities had been permitted to keep would also have to be broken up. He anticipated that the law would also modernize Mexican society by removing what he saw as the twin brakes on the progress of the nation—the conservative clericalism of the Church and the conservative traditionalism of the Indians. His intention was to destroy traditional indigenous communities (and therefore the basis of indigenous societies) and to force Indians to enter the labor market and the mainstream of Mexican society as individuals. His measures did not succeed in abolishing Mexico's huge landholdings—large landowners simply got around the law—and the maldistribution of land was in fact accentuated up until the Mexican revolution (1910–1920). He did succeed in forcing many of Mexico's Indians into the impoverished and landless mass of rural workers, where they gradually lost their indigenous culture.

After the revolution, the government sponsored official policies toward Indians that were known as *indigenismo*. These indigenist policies partially reversed the effects of the reform law because common lands were made available once again to communities (although not solely to indigenous communities). Meanwhile government programs assisted indigenous peoples both economically and through education (there was much debate as to which should have priority) to throw off their backward ways, to divest themselves of their Indianness, and to join the national mainstream. It was hoped that in this way Mexico could finally achieve its destiny as a fully integrated mestizo society. Many indigenous peoples resisted these policies with all the means at their disposal and by the 1980s there was debate in official Mexican circles as to whether their policies of *indigenismo* had failed. They have, in any case, been partially reversed. The new Mexican constitution of 1993 stipulated that Mexico was a pluriethnic nation. Its indigenous peoples are now recognized as having a right to maintain their own ways of life, without being considered outsiders or second class citizens.

This is, at any rate, the theory. What of the practice? The policy of *indigenismo* was predicated on respect for the Indians, while at the same time intending to assimilate them into the Mexican mainstream. What is the rest of the new agenda that permits indigenous groups to retain their cultures within a pluriethnic nation? It is too early to tell, but the recent experience of the Maya in the state of Chiapas may give us some indication.

The Zapatista Rebellion in Chiapas

It is generally known that an "indigenous" uprising took place in Chiapas on January 1, 1994, but exactly what happened, who was involved, and why is very difficult to determine. An analysis of the event, published soon after it took place by a group of scholars who have all worked for years in Chiapas[4] presents the following picture: The redistribution of land, which was one of the important consequences of the Mexican revolution, was never fully carried out in the

---

4. These articles were published together in a special section of the *Cultural Survival Quarterly* (Spring 1994: 9–34) entitled *Why Chiapas?* One of the contributing authors, George Collier, along with Elizabeth L. Quaratiello, has subsequently published in 1994, with a revised version in 1999, an excellent study of the Zapatista rebellion entitled *Basta: Land and the Zapatista Rebellion in Chiapas*.

remote southern state of Chiapas, with its large Maya-speaking indigenous population. During the revolution of 1910–1920, the conservative landowners of Chiapas formed their own private army, known as the raccoons (*Mapaches*), to terrorize the indigenous people of the state. When the two revolutionary leaders Obregón and Carranza were battling for control of Mexico in the final stages of the revolution, the Mapaches of Chiapas supported Obregón. Obregón accepted their support and, when he emerged victorious, turned a blind eye to the fact that land reform was not being fully carried out in Chiapas. Some indigenous communities received common lands known as *ejidos*, which they were supposed to as part of the land reform, but many did not. Meanwhile the landowners used their gunmen to keep the Indians in their place and to protect their own landholdings. These remained substantial because their owners got around the laws limiting the size of their properties by registering them as blocks of small parcels, each "owned" by a different member of a landowner's extended family. In this way Chiapas remained a conservative state controlled by its landowning oligarchy, which had survived the Mexican revolution.

As for the Indians, some indigenous communities, the beneficiaries of land reform, could remain fairly traditional on their common lands. Their leaders were loyal supporters of the PRI, the official party of the revolution. Other Indians were forced to migrate and open up new lands in the jungles of eastern Chiapas. The villages established there were formed not only by landless Maya, but sometimes also by communities of Maya who had converted to Protestantism and been forced out of their traditional villages by the hostility of their Catholic neighbors. These people mostly grew coffee and enjoyed a modest prosperity until the 1970s.

The oil boom of the 1970s changed the government's thinking about the Mexican economy. It began to feel that Mexico did not need and, indeed, could not afford its large population of smallholders, most of them relying on price supports for agriculture and coffee. The revenues coming in from oil would enable the government to restructure the economy and to think of ways to force some of the "inefficient" smallholders out of agriculture altogether. They started to reduce agricultural subsidies and to rethink the whole policy of giving *ejidos* to communities that still had not received them, because they now believed this to be a recipe for spreading poverty throughout the countryside.

It was the changes introduced by then President Salinas in the 1990s that finally set a match to the kindling of rural discontent. Salinas ended the price supports and decreed an end to the *ejidos*. This hit the smallholders of Chiapas particularly hard. They had watched for years while the policies of the revolution were not carried out in

Chiapas, stymied as they were by the big landowners. Some of them had hoped against hope that they would eventually get the *ejidos* to which they were entitled. All of a sudden they were told that there were to be no more *ejidos*, and no more price supports. At the same time, the limits on the size of rural properties, the revolutionary measure that the landowners of Chiapas had systematically flouted, were now officially and greatly increased. It seemed that the big ranchers had now been given license to expand their holdings even further and, in a sense, that the counter-revolution had triumphed.

The sense of betrayal felt by many of the Maya is understandable. Those being forced out of agriculture in this way had unattractive options if they stayed in the state. They could try to get jobs with the detested ranchers or they could try their luck as street vendors. Otherwise they could leave or rebel. Many of them chose to rebel.

The revolt itself was timed to coincide with Mexico's entry into the North American Free Trade Agreement (NAFTA) because the rebels knew how embarrassing it would be for Mexico to crack down on an indigenous rebellion at the precise moment when the country was being welcomed into an exclusive club of the developed nations of North America. As a joke that went the rounds in Mexico City put it, President Salinas went to bed on New Year's eve expecting to wake up the next morning as a North American, but instead he woke up to find himself a Guatemalan. The government did in fact flirt with the "Guatemalan" option of using its overwhelmingly superior military power to squash the rebellion but, although it moved in the army, it decided to negotiate.

The rebels, whose spokesperson was the mysterious, masked figure who called himself Subcommander Marcos, said they were the Zapatista Army of National Liberation, invoking the name of Emiliano Zapata, one of the great leaders and tragic heroes of the revolution. Because Subcommander Marcos did not seem to be an Indian,[5] there was much speculation at first as to whether this was in fact an indigenous uprising at all and, if it was, whether it had been incited by outsiders. The landowners charged that it was all part of a communist conspiracy and that Chiapas had become a theater of action for professional guerillas. Meanwhile Subcommander Marcos showed such a talent for talking to the media and through them to the Mexican people that he became something of a popular hero nationwide. At one time public opinion polls in Mexico City showed that a majority of the population felt that the Zapatistas ought to

---

5. And was subsequently identified as not being one.

enter the political process by founding a new party rather than remaining holed up in their home state.

It seems clear that the rebellion has local roots and that it has attracted considerable outside support, not only in the form of people like Subcommander Marcos but also nationally and even internationally. The Zapatistas chose their moment well, not just to coincide with Mexico's entry into NAFTA, but because they launched their uprising at a time when various crises came together in that country. A downturn in the economy coincided with a crisis of legitimacy for the PRI and for the government. At the same time, the economic measures being adopted by the outgoing Salinas administration seemed to indicate that the government was abandoning not only the peasantry but its entire social agenda. As a result, the Zapatistas, who started out to express the grievances of the Maya in Chiapas, soon found themselves speaking for the poor and the oppressed in a country with huge disparities of income and being urged in some quarters to articulate a new vision for Mexico as a whole.

At the time of writing, the government, still battling its other crises, is in a standoff with the Zapatistas. They have not crushed the rebellion but merely contained it, while negotiations drag on. How does all this affect Mexico's new constitutional determination to be a pluriethnic society? Chiapas, as a backward state which was only partially touched by the revolution of 1910–1920, is admittedly not representative of Mexico as a whole. Nevertheless the events leading up to the Zapatista rebellion do indicate certain tendencies.

The policies of the Salinas administration left people in the rural areas feeling abandoned. Indeed the policies that were put into effect threatened to replicate, one century later, what happened after the reform laws under President Porfírio Diaz. At that time, indigenous communities were broken up and many Indians were forced into the rural proletariat while the large estates grew bigger and the great landlords prospered. Mexico in the 1990s is, of course, very different from the Mexico of the 1890s. It is a country with a sophisticated economy and dynamic industries, but it is not clear whether the "inefficient" smallholders being forced off the land will find any place in the sophisticated sectors of the economy any time soon. In the meantime they remember the postrevolutionary reformist president Lazaro Cárdenas, the redistribution of land through the *ejidos,* and the revolutionary promise to better the lives of the rural poor—and they feel betrayed.

Mexico may now consider itself a pluriethnic society and the government does continue to support programs that foster the sense of separateness and identity of indigenous communities, but those same communities are once again under pressures that threaten to destroy them and to force their inhabitants into the mainstream of the population as a whole.

Brazil

Brazil represents in one sense an opposite extreme. Mexico had a large indigenous population that has only in recent years dwindled to the extent that those who still consider themselves Indians are very much in the minority. Brazil, on the other hand, has always had a very small and sparse indigenous population. Its Portuguese masters soon realized that even their ferociously efficient slavers could not round up enough Indians to do the work on the plantations, so Brazil became the largest importer of African slaves in the western hemisphere. Brazilians, too, have traditionally viewed themselves as a nation founded in racial mixture, but the mix is considered largely a result of mating between Blacks and Whites, with the Indian strain a distant memory from the past. In fact, the Indians themselves were until recently considered to be distant savages beyond the frontiers of settlement.

Even so, Brazil developed its own kind of *indigenismo,* expressed in the indigenist policies pioneered at the beginning of this century by a young army officer, Cândido Mariano Rondon. Rondon, part Indian himself, was a great explorer and in consequence a good friend of President Teddy Roosevelt who, after serving his presidential terms in the United States, actually accompanied Rondon on one of his expeditions into the wilds of central Brazil. Rondon's views about indigenous peoples were, however, quite different from Roosevelt's. He had early on insisted that Indians possessed a capacity for civilization and he was determined to treat them decently. His motto, whenever he traveled through "Indian country" was "Die if need be, but never kill." The results were extraordinary. Rondon's men never killed and they did not die. Instead he institutionalized a technique of making friends with the Indians that was to become the official policy of the SPI (Brazil's Service for the Protection of Indians) created in 1911 with Rondon as its president. The legislation establishing the SPI was extremely liberal for its time and would be considered too radical in many countries of the hemisphere even today. Indigenous peoples were guaranteed the rights to retain their own lands and to maintain their own cultures and the Indian Service was to protect those rights.

This it could never effectively do, which raised a question: Rondon's methods worked very well with Indians at or beyond the frontier, but what happened once the frontier moved forward? This question was answered in the 1960s. Brazil moved its capital inland to Brasilia and its military dictatorship did everything it could to encourage the development of the country's vast hinterland. Indigenous peoples who had hitherto been protected by their remoteness felt the full impact of the advancing frontier. As Indians were killed or dispossessed by the invaders of their traditional lands, Brazil, a nation that took pride in a self-image of encouraging racial mixture rather than racism and of treating its indigenous populations benignly in the spirit of Rondon, was shocked to find itself accused of genocide in the world's press. Though there is no evidence that the government at that time had a policy to exterminate Indians, it did encourage development at all costs and took no measures to protect indigenous peoples from the predictable consequences.

What the government clearly did want was not so much to eliminate the Indians physically as to abolish them socially. So in the 1970s Brazil's official policy toward indigenous peoples became to "emancipate" them. "From what?" demanded indigenous leaders and pro-Indian advocates, pointing out that the Indians were not slaves who could be emancipated from their servile condition. The government made it clear that they were to be emancipated from being Indian. In fact the government put pressure on educated Indians to sign papers declaring themselves "emancipated" and, therefore, no longer Indian. This would prevent them from taking a political role as indigenous leaders and from receiving any of the protections guaranteed to Indians under Brazilian law. The purpose of the legislation was to establish a cutoff point at which Indians, either individually or collectively, could be considered "civilized," therefore no longer Indian, and no longer entitled even in theory to special protection by the Indian service. It did not escape the notice of the Indians and their sympathizers that, if the government succeeded in abolishing Indians in law, then they would no longer be entitled to any protection in fact, and the Indian service would automatically be phased out. Indigenous lands and resources would be that much easier to seize and indigenous societies, deprived of their resource bases, would vanish. The emancipation legislation was never formally approved by the Brazilian parliament. Nevertheless, the Brazilian military has moved in recent years to have indigenous matters treated as issues of national security and therefore referred to them for final arbitration.

Why should the affairs of about 0.2 percent of the Brazilian populational, who were until recently thought of as savages beyond the frontier, come to be treated as a matter of national security? The answer tells us much about the problems faced by indigenous peoples the world over. The military excused the dictatorship that they imposed on Brazil from 1964 to 1985 by arguing that it had saved the country from revolution and enabled it to get on with its economic development. In fact those who criticized the model of development adopted under the military, with its uneven distribution of gain and pain, were considered subversives who might well take up arms against the regime. There had indeed been armed guerilla movements that tried to fight the regime, but they were ruthlessly suppressed.

Nevertheless, the military continues to be on guard against further revolutionary action. Its publications have referred to the unstable politics of Surinam and Guyana and to the volatile combination of insurgency and drug trafficking that have afflicted neighboring Peru and Colombia. Since the drug traffic has now swept into Brazil and the inequalities that might prompt people to revolt have been getting worse in recent years, the military is particularly anxious to prevent any linkage between them.

All these sensitivities implicate the Indians, for many of them live near the nation's frontiers or in areas so remote that guerilla warfare or the drug trade could flourish in them. Furthermore, the concern for safeguarding the ecology of the Amazon basin, which has been so widely expressed internationally, is also held against the Indians. Both the military and the general public in Brazil feel that such concern is hypocritical, especially when expressed by people from nations such as the United States that have grown rich in the past by exploiting their own environment and ignoring sound ecological principles. They also feel it is impertinent, because they consider that the use of the Brazilian Amazon is essentially a matter for Brazilians to decide.

The Indians, then, are considered potential threats to the frontiers or to the security of the state and they are thought to "stand in the way of development" in so far as they impede access to mineral and other resources that are found on the lands they occupy. Finally, the indigenous demand to be allowed to retain their own cultures without being relegated to second class citizenship runs counter to the perception, both public and official, that Brazil is a melting pot country. In 1993 a constitutional convention drew up a new constitution for Brazil as a somewhat delayed marker of the country's passage from dictatorship to democracy.[6]

A provision of that constitution would have declared Brazil, like Mexico, to be a "pluriethnic nation" and thus guaranteed the right of indigenous peoples to maintain their own cultures, but it was voted down.

The Yanomami[7]

In the 1980s Brazil found itself once more being pilloried in the world's press for mistreating its indigenous populations, in particu-

---

6. The last military president stepped down in 1985.
7. The materials in this section are drawn from press reports in the files of Cultural Survival, from the bulletins of the Commission for the Creation of the Yanomami Park, and especially from the concluding chapters of Alcida Ramos's recent book *Sanumá Memories*.

lar the Yanomami. A consideration of what has happened to the Yanomami since the 1970s is therefore a good way to examine the
relation between the theory and practice of Brazilian *indigenismo.*

Yanomami is the generic name used for the peoples living on both
sides of the border between Brazil and Venezuela and speaking Yanomam, Yanomam, Yanam, and Sanumá, languages that are more or
less mutually intelligible. It is estimated that there were about 10,000
Yanomami at the beginning of the 1980s, making them perhaps the
largest relatively isolated group still living according to their traditional ways in the Amazonian rainforest. The comparative isolation of
the Brazilian Yanomami[8] came to an end in the 1970s when the military government sponsored a road-building program to open up the
interior of the country. Together with the Transamazon Highway,
which ran south of the Amazon River, they started building another
highway known as the Northern Perimeter, which passed right
through the territory of the Yanomami. This highway was left incom-
plete for lack of funds or perhaps lack of interest, but the penetration
of Yanomami territory and the colonization project that went with it
brought disease, starvation, and death to the Indians of the region. As
Alcida Ramos commented bitterly: "Millions of dollars were wasted
on a road that fell short of its purpose and destination. All it achieved
was the conquest of a portion of the Yanomami, through death, social
turmoil and land expropriation" (Ramos 1995: 274).

Worse was to come. Gold miners started coming to the region in
the mid-seventies, and by 1980 there was a full-fledged gold rush in
progress. At this time the federal government was still making ges-
tures to protect the Indians. It had abolished the SPI in the 1970s and
replaced it with FUNAI (The National Indian Foundation), which
was supposed to correct the abuses of the old Indian service, protect
the lands and resources of indigenous peoples, and provide them
with education and health care. FUNAI, however, regularly lacked
the funds to carry out its mandate. In the Yanomami case, FUNAI did
occasionally call in the federal police to try to expel the miners from
Indian territory. On one occasion they had to come to the rescue of a
FUNAI post that was being besieged by a uniformed contingent of
gunmen in the pay of the miners.

Friends of the Yanomami, led by the CCPY (Commission for the
Creation of a Yanomami Park) were by this time lobbying hard for the
creation, demarcation, and protection of a continuous tract of territory

---

8. I only discuss the Brazilian Yanomami in this section, so it should be
    understood that henceforward all references to Yanomami refer only to those
    living in Brazil.

that would be a Yanomami reserve. The idea was, however, opposed by a combination of powerful forces—the miners, the state of Roraima, which had no interest in seeing a large tract of its territory cordoned off for indigenous peoples, and above all, the military. These interests consistently supported a counter-proposal, the so-called archipelago plan that would establish a rash of small Yanomami reserves in this remote region. Anthropologists critical of this plan argued that it would mean the extinction of the Yanomami.

A turning point in the Yanomami situation was reached in 1986. That was when the military dramatically enlarged a small airstrip that had previously been used by FUNAI and local missionaries. The new airstrip, which came to be known by the Yanomami name for the site, *Paapiu,* was part of the military's Calha Norte (Northern Drainage) Project, which had been kept secret up until that time. This project was intended to establish a significant military presence along the Amazon frontiers, to protect Brazilian territory from encroachment, to facilitate its colonization by Brazilians, and to establish "discipline" in the newly colonized areas, which meant guarding against drug-trafficking and subversion, including subversion of Brazil's national security by Indian or pro-Indian groups.

The immediate effect of the new airstrip was to intensify the gold rush into Yanomami country. Gold miners poured in. Planes were arriving and taking off from Paapiu all through the daylight hours. The roar of their engines hovered over Paapiu like a pall, while the surrounding jungles reverberated with the racket of mining machinery. The authorities knew very well what effect this would have on the Yanomami, for the military declared the region to be an area of national security. The missionaries who had been giving medical assistance to the Yanomami were told to leave. So were anthropologists and other researchers. Access was restricted to miners, the military, and the Indian service, which was now working under orders from the military. The agency's task had become that of ensuring that the Indians did not interfere with the gold mining and that pro-Indian witnesses were not allowed access to the region.

It was nearly two years before journalists managed to get into Paapiu and what they saw horrified them. One quarter of the Yanomami in the region were already dead. The majority of the rest were desperately sick, and many were starving and emaciated. They were particularly moved by the plight of starving and orphaned Yanomami children. Their reports provoked an international outcry and the Brazilian government hastily set up an emergency medical program for the Yanomami, but government policy remained essentially unchanged. The president now claimed that it was physically impossible to expel the miners from Yanomami territory. After all, there were tens of thousands of them there, all armed to the teeth.

The federal police were not strong enough to evict them. The state and its authorities were squarely on the side of the miners, and the army was unwilling to do such a messy job. In any case, President Samey soon showed where his sympathies lay. In his lame duck period, before the next president was sworn in, he issued a decree for the demarcation of three reserves in Yanomami territory, not for the Indians (those were still being debated), but for the goldminers!

His successor, President Collor, now bore the brunt of international criticism concerning the treatment of the Yanomami and also the runaway pollution of land and water as a result of the uncontrolled mining operations. Collor won praise for ordering the mining operations to cease and having the airstrips (there were now many of them) dynamited. Few newspapers outside of Brazil noted, however, that the airstrips were soon repaired and the miners back at work again. Collor was less responsive to the military than Samey and more anxious to improve Brazil's international image, especially on the eve of the world ecological conference, held in Rio de Janeiro in 1992, but he faced the same dilemma as his predecessor. A gold rush is as hard to stop as a herd of stampeding buffalo. The miners were many, well armed and well connected, both politically and with the very drug traffickers who were the supposed targets of military vigilance in the north (Ramos 1995: 288). When their airstrips were destroyed, they quietly repaired them. They were openly supported by the state authorities and tacitly supported by the army. The Yanomami were few and dying out rapidly. Their support came from pro-Indian activists and segments of public opinion in Brazil, backed up by international organizations, all of whom were horrified by the ongoing genocide.

The unequal contest still continues. There have been some successes. In 1991, for example, President Collor, at long last, signed a decree setting aside a contiguous tract of territory as a Yanomami reserve, albeit a much smaller one than originally requested. But the reserve is neither demarcated nor protected and the miners still ride roughshod over the Yanomami. In fact, two years after the reserve had been formally decreed, a group of Brazilian miners carried out a horrifying massacre of sixteen Yanomami in a village just across the border in Venezuela. The killings were carried out with the utmost brutality. The victims, mostly children, were stabbed and beheaded and the killers never brought to justice, in spite of the outcry that the massacre produced. It is understandable, then, that Alcida Ramos's recent book on the Sanumá/Yanomami ends on a note of lament as she writes: "I didn't expect to be around, only ten years after my immersion into an autonomous and healthy culture such as I found among the Sanumá, to see one of the worst examples of cultural devastation in the recent history of Brazilian Indigenism." (Ramos 1955: 312)

Conclusion

These two cases—Mexico and Brazil—are very different. Mexico contained a large indigenous population whose "backwardness" was felt to impede the modernization of the country. This view of Indian "backwardness" and its doleful effect on the nation was shared by the Hispanic elites of all the countries in Latin America that also had large indigenous populations (Guatemala, El Salvador, Ecuador, Peru, and Bolivia). In all these countries it was felt that they could only modernize to the extent that their indigenous masses gave up (or were deprived of) their native cultures.

Only in Peru, at the turn of this century during a period of national soul searching about the country's backwardness, were there influential voices that argued for the continuation of indigenous cultures. José Carlos Mariátegui, the nation's most famous theorist of the left, argued that the country should modernize by incorporating the Indians into national life and reinstituting some kind of Incaic socialism. He was referring to the system that operated in the Inca empire at the time when the Spanish destroyed it in the mid-sixteenth century. The Inca was an absolute ruler whose subjects owed him service, including military service, and tribute. In return the empire offered protection from want, since the granaries maintained by the state were opened to the people when they were afflicted by poor harvests or other natural disasters. Mariátegui's ideas were never taken seriously as a political program in his time, but there is still nostalgic talk of Incaic socialism in Peru. Meanwhile Victor Haya de la Torre, probably Peru's most famous recent leftist politician (though he was never elected to the presidency), went even further and argued that the future not only of Peru but of all the Americas depended on the coming of a truly Indian revolution. Peru was an exception in having such ideas advanced by leading intellectuals and politicians, but even in Peru these ideas were never translated into policies. On the contrary, Haya de la Torre abandoned his youthful enthusiasm for an Indian future when he discovered that there were no votes in it.

Mexico has now broken with this age-old tradition of insisting that its indigenous people assimilate. By declaring itself to be pluriethnic,[9] it has indicated that its indigenous peoples have a legitimate place in the nation without having to give up their Indianness; but, as we saw, those same peoples are still facing very strong pressures that threaten to destroy their indigenous identities.

---

9. As have Bolivia, Ecuador, Peru, and Colombia.

By contrast, in Brazil the Indians have for a long time been an insignificant and marginal presence in the life of the nation. Their very marginality makes them classic examples of indigenous peoples, yet that marginality does not protect them. They are considered potentially subversive, a danger to the nation's frontiers, obstacles to development, and a threat to the state, which is why the government has been trying to get rid of them.

ETHNOCIDE: THE COUNTER-ARGUMENTS

States regularly justify their attempts to eradicate indigenous cultures with a series of arguments. The invaders of the Americas argued at first that the indigenous peoples were not fully human. Because they lacked the essential attributes of humanity—souls or a belief in Christianity—they were not entitled to what we would nowadays call "human rights" and were certainly thought to be in need of education to make them see the error of their ways and to induce them to abandon them. Later, the mission of conquest was justified in evolutionary terms. The conquerors brought civilization to the backward natives, if only the latter could be forced or induced to accept it. Nowadays some people may be hesitant to insist on the civilizing mission of the powerful. The grim history of the twentieth century has made us wary of such claims. Development, however, is another matter. Indigenous peoples are usually accused of standing in the way of development, and that is normally sufficient grounds for dispossessing them and destroying their ways of life. If they are unable or unwilling to abandon their separate identities and disappear into the mainstream of the nations in which they live, they are also said to undermine the state and to impede modernization. Hence, it is argued, indigenous cultures must disappear. Sometimes we are told that the disappearance of such archaic cultures may be regrettable, but that it is also inevitable, since they cannot survive in the modern world. In short, stronger societies are bound to extinguish weaker ones and there is not much that can be done about it, since this is the result of some sort of Darwinian process where only the fittest survive.

These arguments are plausible and they are certainly part of the conventional wisdom today, but they are false. We would do well to remember here that it was not only Sepúlveda who argued before the king of Spain in 1550 that slavery was part of the human condition and that indigenous peoples were destined for it. As recently as the nineteenth century scholars were quoting learned arguments to the effect that the differences in the natural endowments of individuals and races, coupled with the unavoidable differences of power in human affairs, made slavery inevitable. We now realize that those arguments were false, although widely believed. How about some of the false-hoods that are widely believed in our own day?

Consider the argument that indigenous peoples must abandon their cultures because they are "backward" and, for good measure, that they "stand in the way of development." What exactly does this mean? Usually that they do things of which governments disapprove. The few remaining nomadic peoples left on earth are a case in point.

Nomads[10]

The prejudice against nomads is very old. It is true that sedentary peoples have often envied their freedom and their political independence and even idealized their simplicity and their poverty; more often, nomads have been hated and feared. Nomads could use their mobility as a strategic resource, enabling them to prey on their settled neighbors. The Mongols did this so effectively in the thirteenth and fourteenth centuries that they conquered China, the Near East, and eastern Europe before their empire broke up. Even smaller and less-organized groups of nomads could control the resources of important trade routes, such as salt in Africa or silk in Asia.

The days of nomad power are long gone, but the prejudice against them persists. Their way of life, their diffuseness, and their mobility seem strange and awkward. They are also inconvenient to nation-states: as groups they straddle national boundaries and disrupt the imaginary map of homogenous national identities. They live in unpleasant places, where it is very cold, barren, too hot, or too "far" from the centers of our cosmopolitan world.

Nomad societies lack the capacity for unlimited expansion that agricultural societies possess. Nomad populations tend to remain constant over long periods of time; agricultural populations, in favorable conditions, explode. There are clear reasons for this. The balance between people and animals, and between animals and resources that feed (and water) them, is precarious among mobile populations, who must constantly strive to maintain this balance. As a Somali saying runs, "Abundance and scarcity are never far apart; the rich and the poor frequent the same house."

Nomads have been forced by circumstances to stay in tune with their environment. Their very survival depends on it. It is, therefore, especially ironic that modern environmental disasters are routinely blamed on them. Drought and famine on an unprecedented scale

---

10. This section is excerpted from Maybury-Lewis 1992.

have recently decimated nomad populations and the herds on which they depend, especially in Africa. Yet nomadic pastoralists of both East and West Africa are accused by their governments and by earnest development agencies of degrading the soil and helping the deserts encroach on the farmlands at their edges. They are said to do this by overgrazing. Nomads normally own common rights in pasture land; it is therefore supposed by outsiders that, because this land is a resource available to all, it is the responsibility of no one in particular. The theory goes that nomads refuse to limit the size of their herds or to accept any limitations on their movements, with the result that they destroy their own environment and enlarge the desert. A publication of the Food and Agriculture Organization of the United Nations (cited in Horowitz 1979) was fierce in its criticism of West African nomads at a time when a terrible drought was ravaging the region. They were said to be a social, economic, and political burden on their respective countries—people who take care of nothing, shun all manual work, refuse to pay their taxes, are reluctant to sell their animals, and fail to make the economic contribution to countries that their governments have a right to expect.

In fact, nomads take elaborate care of their grazing lands. If they are reluctant to sell their animals, this is not, as bureaucrats think, because they are irrational, but rather because they understand the necessities of pastoralism better than city dwellers do. They know how many animals they need as a safeguard against emergencies, and they keep them, in spite of the calculations of outside experts. They keep steers, too, that city folk think should be slaughtered for meat because they can no longer be used for breeding; but this too makes sense because herding is labor intensive and steers help keep the herd together.

One of the few remaining nomadic peoples of Eastern Africa are the Gabra, who live in northern Kenya (see map on p. xiii). Space travelers who touched down in Gabra country might wonder if they had landed on the wrong planet, for the limitless red expanses of the Chalbi Desert seem more like Mars than our own green earth. But the Gabra consider this wilderness their land, and they see it as a place of freedom and fertility. There is water for those who know where to look, good grasses and bad grasses, and protective trees standing like shrines under the sheltering sky. Above all, it is a good land for camels, and it is their camels that define the Gabra.

Gabra keep cattle and goats, but they may be tended by herders as far away as two hundred miles from the community. The camp travels with the camels as the animals meander through and around the Chalbi Desert, constantly moving on in search of forage or to get away from their own dung. The aversion to dung is not just a whim on the part of these notoriously whimsical beasts, for ticks collect in the dung and make the camels' lives miserable. They may even do worse than that, for the ticks sometimes carry a disease that can be fatal to camels. So the camels must move and the people with them.

If possible, the Gabra pick a new site that can be reached in a day, to avoid spending a night in the open with their huts and all their possessions loaded on their camels. They are not averse, however, to moving fifty miles or more when necessary. Every eight years or so they make pilgrimages over long distances to their sacred sites in southern Ethiopia, where Gabra men go through the ceremonies that enable them to graduate from one age-set to the next. On such journeys the community must camp out, building thorn fences for their smaller animals, while the camels, cattle, and the Gabra themselves sleep out under the enveloping skies.

But there is drama even in routine migrations. People become restless once the decision to move has been made, and women often get up in the middle of the night to begin dismantling their households. If there is no moon, they have to do this by touch in the darkness, which is possible because everything in the household has its place and is packed and loaded in a certain order. The men tie upright poles onto the camels and the women then roll up everything in the household, even the outer skins of the huts themselves, and pack them between the poles. The poles are then bound together and lashed tight by ropes on the camel. All the packing and loading is done entirely by women. Men take no part in it other than to restrain the camels if they become unruly or to help lift some item that is too heavy for the women.

Gabra live their entire lives in these unending cycles of migration. The movement is necessary in order to live off their land, but the Gabra love their desert and see it as a supportive environment where people like themselves can live with dignity. They know how to use their land and conserve its resources. They move even before they are forced to in order to ensure that the land is replenished for the future. So, when the rains come they leave their dry season pastures and move to the highlands. They could stay where they are, but then the area would be overgrazed when the dry season came around again.

They manage their pastures by setting controlled fires to drive back the bush. Because their herds soon denude an area of edible grasses, leaving only unpalatable ones, Gabra burn off the bad grasses to allow the good ones to flourish in the ash. They are also careful of trees. Full-grown acacia trees are protected, for example, and called "bulls," for they regenerate the landscape just as bulls regenerate the herd; another tree, whose supple branches make it particularly useful for hut construction, is also protected against overexploitation; and trees whose spreading roots stabilize underground water sources are considered sacred and treated as shrines.

This sense of the sacred permeates the Gabra landscape and protects it. Aneesa Kassam, who studies the Gabra, writes that their philosophy of life can be summed up in their idea of *finn*, meaning fertility and plenty. The sky god sends rain to bless the earth, make the grass grow, and ensure that animals and humans have enough to eat and grow fat. *Finn* is the earth and the cycle of life that takes place on it. Human beings contribute to *finn* as they care for the earth and for their animals, as they exchange livestock, nourish friendships, exchange ideas, tell tales, or sing songs. They and their wanderings are part of a constant cycle of creation and replenishment.

Not too long ago, the Gabra were briefly the victims of well-intentioned experts. While Kenya was still a British colony, the authorities decided to prohibit the Gabra from burning their grasslands in the old-fashioned way. The result was a buildup of deadwood that caused a huge fire that raged out of control and destroyed a large part of the forest on Marsabit Mountain. Since then, the Gabra's own small controlled fires have been looked on as a useful and intelligent practice. Nowadays Kenyan ranchers use the Gabra combination of camel browsing and range burning to keep the grasslands under control.

In part because of vindications like this one, the Kenyan government has begun to realize that taking the nomads off the land is not necessarily a wise thing to do and may even become a process of ecological degradation. It has become clear that, if the deserts of Africa are spreading, it is not because of the nomads and their way of life—for their survival has always depended on cultivating a harmonious relationship with their environment. The fault is more likely to lie in efforts to squeeze the "economic contributions that their governments have a right to expect" out of regions that have traditionally been used by nomadic herders.

In short, it is the settled populations and the governments who represent them who are more likely to cause desertification (not the nomads) and they do it in the name of "development." Such "development" often has harmful consequences that affect everybody, but it is especially disastrous for indigenous peoples, because planners neglect or scorn their knowledge and so belittle one of humankind's greatest attributes—adaptability. Humans can live almost anywhere, given ecological knowledge and the appropriate social relations. The best development planning takes account of both the interests and the expertise of those in the areas to be "developed." Where this is done—and it can be (see Maybury-Lewis 1992: 35–62)—indigenous peoples do not suffer needlessly from a development in which they have had no say.

Backwardness and Cultural Survival

Peoples who practice swidden agriculture are also considered backward. This method (often called slash-and-burn agriculture) involves burning off the undergrowth and clearing a field for planting. Such fields are only used for a year or two before the cultivator moves on and repeats the process elsewhere. Swidden agricultors may move in a rough circle and come back to their original fields after they have lain fallow for some years. They are accused of being ecologically destructive, yet studies have shown that their method is a sustainable form of low-input, low-yield agriculture, which is less destructive of the environment than many of the intensive methods used by more "civilized" peoples.

Those considered most backward of all are the peoples who live by hunting and gathering, supplemented by some agriculture. Very few peoples practice no agriculture at all and they are invariably those who live in extreme climates, such as the Inuit (Eskimo) or the traditional Aborigines of Australia's central deserts. Hunters and gatherers are not normally accused of destroying the environment, which would anyway be absurd because they treat the natural world with a respect that more "civilized" people have long ago abandoned.

The "backwardness" of these peoples lies not so much in what they do as what they do not do. They do not produce big surpluses and therefore do not participate in the economic systems that encroach on them. Accordingly, state policies toward them all over the world stress the need to "bring them into the twenty-first century." To do this, it is often felt necessary to develop not only their lands but also their attitudes.

This is clearly shown by a remarkable consistency in the attitudes of all the invaders of the Americas. Whether they were Protestant or Catholic, English, French, Dutch, Spanish, or Portuguese, they were uniformly outraged by those indigenous societies that did not recognize private property, particularly the private ownership of land. The invaders felt vaguely (but quite correctly) that this was the basis of civilization as they knew it, and they expended enormous effort in trying to stamp out the communitarian beliefs and practices of indigenous peoples, whom they deemed backward for subscribing to them. At the present time, indigenous societies that believe it is immoral not to share with one's kin or with those less fortunate than oneself are also considered backward, for this surely hampers capital accumulation and therefore "progress" as the modern world defines it.

It is rarely argued that "backward" societies should be destroyed because their practices are morally reprehensible. Often these societies have been stigmatized as backward in the first place for practicing in their public lives the sharing, thrift, communalism, and so on that the modern world has relegated to being private virtues that should not be allowed to interfere with the expansive and accumulative tendencies of modern economies. Why, then, should such societies be destroyed? Here two arguments are usually offered. First, such societies are said to be doomed to extinction anyway because they cannot survive in the modern world. Second, they stand in the way of development. Civilizing them will thus encourage development and do a favor to indigenous individuals, who can join the modern world once they are freed from their archaic ways. It is true that hunters and gatherers cannot go on living that way if their lands are invaded and their game driven away. Nomads cannot continue their wandering ways if others move in on their grazing lands, and so on. It is therefore a reasonable question to ask how such cultures can hope to survive.

The question contains some hidden assumptions, however. It assumes that a culture or way of life cannot survive if the bearers of that culture have to change their ways of making a living. It also assumes that traditional societies cannot change and that, if they did, they could not be said to have survived, for they would no longer be what they once were. But all societies in the world are in a constant process of change. Change of itself does not destroy a culture. In fact, we expect modern societies to change. It is part of their modernity that they do so. Do their cultures therefore vanish? Americans in the United States no longer live on farms and ride around on horseback the way they did when the founding fathers wrote the constitution, yet it is generally recognized that there is some continuity between the American culture of those times and the American culture of the present. Cultural survival is not a matter of maintaining a way of life frozen at a certain moment as if it were in a time warp. It is a matter of a society's having enough confidence in its past and enough say in its future to be able to maintain the spirit of its culture through all the changes that it will inevitably undergo. From this perspective, it is clear that the stereotype of indigenous cultures being bound to disappear because they cannot deal with the modern world is quite wrong. Indigenous societies have shown themselves to be extraordinarily resilient in maintaining the spirit of their cultures through dramatic changes. Indigenous cultures only disappear if the bearers of the culture are scattered or annihilated by external force, or when drastic changes are forcibly and rapidly imposed on indigenous societies, rendering them unable to cope. The point to remember is that indigenous cultures are not extinguished by natural laws but by political processes that are susceptible to human control. To argue otherwise is to obscure the fact that indigenous peoples are victims of the convenient use of power against the relatively powerless. Arguments that make the destruction of indigenous cultures seem natural and even beneficial (in terms of modernization) preempt the discussion of possible alternatives and thus contribute to the inevitability of that destruction.

The Supposed Threat to the State

There is another line of argument that maintains that indigenous cultures should not be allowed to endure because they undermine the state. This will be discussed more fully in Chapter 4, but needs to be mentioned briefly here. This argument normally means that, if indigenous cultures are legitimated within the state, this would alter the social order in ways that the elite would find unacceptable. This is not the same thing as "undermining the state," although the elites would certainly have us think so. As we saw earlier, Mariátegui called in the 1920s for Peru to recognize and celebrate its indigenous roots. The idea was forcefully opposed by those in power because it would have involved changes amounting to a social revolution. On the other hand, indigenous societies with comparatively small populations are said to undermine the state because, if their right to be different is accepted, then that would change the nature of melting pot states.

Alternatively, indigenous societies are said to threaten the state by wishing to secede from it, yet the majority of indigenous peoples who are demanding their rights today have no interest in secession. What they ask for is a recognition of their rights *within the state*. Ironically, it is more usual for states to shift position than for the indigenous peoples at their edges to do so. Maps are redrawn (or sometimes drawn for the first time) that divide up indigenous peoples between states, or assign them to this state or that with little consideration of their past history or of their relations with local rulers. Under these circumstances, the conventional accusation that indigenous peoples at the frontiers are anxious to secede is often a classic example of projection (imputing to others what is running through one's own mind). There are, of course, some indigenous groups that have made their desire to secede quite clear and they will be discussed later. The point is that such desires are regularly imputed to the majority of indigenous societies who have no such wishes, in order to avoid having to deal with their genuine demands for local autonomy.

At the heart of the prejudice against indigenous societies are the twin issues of modernization and development. States feel they cannot modernize effectively if they tolerate indigenous cultures in their midst. They feel even more that they cannot exploit the resources that lie within their territories if access to them is impeded by indigenous peoples. In the next sections, I shall discuss these contentions with the aid of specific examples.

INDIA: WHERE INDIGENOUS IS SCHEDULED[11]

The government of India has taken a firm position on indigenous peoples, insisting that there are none in India or, more precisely, that

---

11. The materials in this section are drawn from von Fürer-Haimendorf 1982 and Fisher 1995.

there are none who can reasonably be singled out as indigenous, because most of the peoples of the subcontinent have been there for thousands of years. It is also true, however, that there have always been independent tribal societies in India, living in remote regions at the margins of established kingdoms and states. These peoples were traditionally taken for granted as inhabiting the world of hills and forests beyond settled society. So long as there was little population pressure on the land, the tribal peoples were largely left to their own devices, but this began to change under the influence of British administration in the nineteenth century. The population of India was growing and the establishment of the *Pax Britannica* throughout the country meant that it was increasingly safe for outsiders to venture into what had hitherto been regarded as tribal territory. As a result, settlers started to move in and they soon acquired legal title to large tracts of tribal land. The process was facilitated unintentionally by the government, which insisted on applying systems of land tenure and taxation in tribal areas that were unfamiliar to the local people and ran counter to their traditional customs. It was the incoming settlers who profited from the official system at the expense of the traditional landholders. There was only one part of British India where local invaders did not encroach on tribal lands and that was in the hill regions of the northeast, close to what is now the border with Burma (see map on p. xiv). This was a land of rugged mountains and narrow valleys that had never been penetrated by the peoples who lived on the plains of Assam, especially because it was occupied by peoples such as the Naga, the Apa Tani, the Nishi, and the Mishmi who all had a warrior reputation. Their lands were, however, invaded by the British themselves, who declared large areas of the hills to be Crown territory and leased them out for tea planting and logging, while the remainder was left for the exclusive use of the tribal peoples.

The constitution adopted by the newly independent Republic of India in 1950 recognized the marginal peoples of the subcontinent as *scheduled tribes* and required each state to prepare lists of such tribes and to report on them periodically to the central government. At present, there are more than 50 million people, or close to 8 percent of the population of India, who belong to the scheduled tribes, of which there are more than two hundred, speaking over one hundred languages. In the northeast of India they are the majority populations in the newly created "tribal" states of Arunachal Pradesh, Mizoram, and Nagaland, but the vast majority of scheduled tribes live as minorities in the central states of Bihar, Orissa, and Madhya Pradesh.

The constitution established special protections for scheduled tribes and also specified that they should receive certain benefits. In 1993, for instance, 41 seats out of 545 were reserved for their representatives in the national parliament and 527 out of a total of 4,061 in the state legislatures. Places were reserved for members of scheduled tribes in government service and even in private enterprise, and a series of laws was passed, prohibiting the transfer of lands from tribals to non-tribals in scheduled areas. These laws were not effectively implemented, however, so the alienation of tribal lands continued. Invaders of scheduled areas could usually count on the connivance, if not the actual support, of local officials, who took their side against the "backward peoples" whom the officials were supposed in law to protect.

Nowadays these laws are flouted quite openly. For example, in 1991 the supreme court of India outlawed dolomite mining in the 200,000-acre Sariska reserve in Rajasthan, but more than 300 mines continue in operation and the government of Rajasthan continues to grant new mining leases. Meanwhile local forestry officials, who collaborate with the mining department to keep the mines functioning, levy fines for cutting down trees against the Meena tribal people who live on the reserve. In Bihar and Orissa states the steady alienation of tribal lands has deprived the scheduled tribes of their access to resources and created severe famine among them. These are not isolated instances, but are part of a pattern of "development" being inflicted on tribal peoples.

In general, the development strategies pursued by state governments have deprived tribal peoples of their lands and resources and reduced them to poverty or actual starvation. In the name of environmental protection, forestry officials prevent tribal peoples from collecting the forest products they traditionally relied on, thus slowly forcing them off their lands. In other areas the methods are more direct.

In northeastern India, for example, the Nagas had asked to be allowed to form their own independent state when the British withdrew in 1947. They signed an agreement with India under the terms of which the Nagas should have local autonomy under Indian trusteeship for ten years and then should be allowed to choose whether they would remain in India. In 1951 a plebiscite held in Nagaland showed that a large majority of Nagas wanted independence. In 1954 India invaded Nagaland and divided Naga territory between the newly created Indian state of Nagaland and the states of Assam, Arunachal, and Manipur, hoping in this way to split the Naga and weaken their independence movement while at the same time giving them a Naga state where they could maintain their own traditions. The Nagas were not satisfied and continue to demand that the lands taken from them by the British be returned to them, that the Naga-inhabited areas be joined together in one contiguous Naga land and that Nagas should have the right to determine their own future within this territory. The Indian government's response has so far been a military one. The Indian army occupies all Naga-inhabited regions, and has been fighting secessionist guerillas for fifty years. By some estimates India keeps about two hundred thousand troops in the area in order to deal with two and a half million Naga (there are another half million Naga across the border in Burma). Meanwhile the bulk of the Naga population is becoming increasingly embittered by Indian repression and human rights abuses. This costly stalemate has led some Indian generals to state publicly that India should come to an agreement with the Nagas and stop the conflict. Unfortunately, this is politically difficult for India to do now. It would have been relatively easy to grant limited or even full autonomy to the Nagas in the 1950s, but currently there are separatist movements fighting for independence in other parts of India, such as Kashmir or the Punjab, where radical Sikhs are demanding their own separate state. Negotiating Naga autonomy is, therefore, fraught with political danger now, which is in all probability why the Indians persevere with the protracted and costly struggle. The Naga stalemate is a classic instance of an indigenous peoples' being denied their rights for reasons having to do with the security of frontiers and the politics of the nation-state.

The other major argument used against indigenous peoples is, as we have seen, that they stand in the way of development. This is the reasoning behind perhaps the largest and certainly the most dramatic government program to affect tribal peoples in India, namely the massive Sardar Sarovar project, involving the damming of the Narmada river. The purpose of the project was to irrigate arid regions of western India in the states of Gujarat and Rajasthan and to bring drinking water to Gujarat. Supporters of the project argued that it would potentially benefit some 25 to 40 million people. Opponents insisted that the benefits had been much exaggerated and the environmental and human costs minimized. It was in any case certain that it would flood the homes of at least 100,000 people, many, if not most, of whom were tribal.

The project became the focus of intense controversy involving the World Bank and the Japanese government, who were initially backing it, together with agencies of the government of India and of the states of Gujarat, Maharashtra, and Madhya Pradesh. It was strongly opposed by environmentalists and human rights activists both in India and abroad, who in turn helped to organize the protests of the people who faced relocation and might otherwise not have known how to fight it. Eventually the World Bank commissioned an independent review of the project that was very critical of it; the Japanese government cut off its funding for it and the government of India, anticipating that the World Bank would also stop funding it, announced that it would accept no more World Bank funds and would complete the project at its own expense.

There are many lessons that can be learned from a study of this project and its problems, but here I shall focus only on its tribal aspect. Initial opposition to the project was driven by a real concern for the human rights of the poor and the marginal who were about to be driven from their homes and their land, with little warning and inadequate forethought. It was pointed out that there had been a great deal of technical planning for the project but grossly inadequate social planning for the compensation and resettlement of the people who would be flooded out. The authors of the independent review further added that the cultural uniqueness of the tribal peoples who were to be displaced entitled them to special consideration from both the World Bank and the government of India. This sentiment was criticized by the Narmada Control Authority as a deplorable attempt to create a rift among scheduled castes (those who used to be called the "untouchables" in the Hindu caste system), scheduled tribes, and the rest of Indian society.

The reaction of the Authority obscures the fact that a gulf does exist between scheduled tribes and the rest of Indian society. Their cultures are different from the mainstream. Their rights, particularly to land and other natural resources, are rarely recognized in law. In fact the tribal peoples in the Narmada project area were often referred to by the state governments as "thieves" because, in living off lands to which they had never been granted titles of ownership, they "stole" resources that properly belonged to the government. In this view, as the tribals themselves remarked in disgust, they were not acknowledged as having any rights to the resources off which they traditionally lived. They were thought to be like monkeys, who were simply expected to move to higher ground when their habitat was flooded.

As the battle over the project raged, the various agencies supporting it found themselves trying to give better and more specific guarantees concerning relocation and compensation to those whom they were going to move. Here, again, the tribal peoples posed special problems. By law they were entitled to special consideration, but that made their relocation more expensive than it might otherwise have been. Reducing the number of tribals in the project area therefore saved money, so there was considerable incentive to insist that people who claimed to be tribals (and who had no titles to land as a result) were not really tribal at all, because traits from Hindu society could be detected in their cultures. At the same time, the compensation of those who were admittedly tribal posed a problem, for what would be fair compensation for the loss of lands and resources to which they had no acknowledged titles in the first place?

The project is not yet completed and the story is not finished, but it has graphically illustrated the problems faced by tribal peoples in

India. In sum, India has, since independence, recognized the special situation of its scheduled tribes and has offered them theoretical protection in law. There has not, however been much enthusiasm at the local levels for applying the law. On the contrary, invaders of tribal lands, whether they are farmers or miners or distant entrepreneurs, have regularly found that local authorities are sympathetic to them and unwilling to champion the rights of tribal peoples. Nor is it only the authorities at the lowest levels who take this attitude, as the whole saga of the Narmada dam shows. The ideology, politics, and corruption that all come together under the rubric of development are usually too powerful for tribal peoples and their sympathizers to resist.

SOUTHEAST ASIA AND INDONESIA: INDIGENOUS PEOPLES AND ETHNIC MINORITIES[12]

Southeast Asia shares with India (see map on p. xiv) the characteristic that every state in the region contains a plethora of ethnic groups. In some cases, as with the Orang Asli (literally "original people") of Malaysia, there is no doubt that these are indigenous groups. They have been there since time immemorial and are marginal to and dominated by a state that is alien to them. In other parts of Southeast Asia, relatively large populations may be considered "tribal" and marginal to the state, whereas geographically remote populations may function as ethnic minorities within the nation, showing that the distinction between an indigenous people and an ethnic minority is also a function of that group's relationship to the state.

It must be remembered that the states of Southeast Asia (with the exception of Siam, now Thailand) were colonial creations and even the present borders of Thailand have much to do with the relations between it and the contending colonial powers that surrounded it. It was therefore in the nineteenth century, under the aegis of the colonial powers, that the present-day states acquired their borders and the mix of peoples that make up their populations.

Since then, the independent states of Southeast Asia have differed dramatically from each other in ideology and internal organization, yet they have shown a marked similarity in their attitudes and policies toward the tribal peoples within their borders. The state in each case has seen itself as representing a nation, which is, in Benedict Anderson's phrase, an "imagined community" (Anderson 1983) in

---

12. The materials in this section are largely drawn from Cultural Survival 1987.

which certain peoples relate to each other in certain ways in order to carry forward the national agenda. Tribal peoples are considered outsiders to this national community. The nations in their turn, although differing dramatically among themselves, resemble each other in that they all strive to eradicate the distinctive identities and ways of life of their tribal peoples.

Because tribal peoples are considered outsiders, they do not have the same rights as ordinary citizens. They normally lack rights to land and resources and the swidden or slash-and-burn agriculture that they regularly practice has been banned by all the governments of mainland Southeast Asia. These bans are justified as measures taken in defense of local ecology, but because other ecologically more harmful activities are permitted to mainstream villagers or logging and mining companies, it is clear that the bans are intended as much to eliminate tribal ways of life as they are to protect the ecosystem.

Furthermore, because tribal peoples are considered outsiders, they are treated similarly by relatively open and democratic regimes as they are by relatively closed and authoritarian ones. In the Philippines, for example, tribal peoples face a situation similar to that in India. Their rights to land and resources are protected by a maze of legislation, but the elites and their political allies regularly find ways to circumvent the laws and to seize or otherwise use tribal lands. This is often done with the aid or connivance of the courts and the military. Nor is it only the elites that can do this successfully. In some parts of the Philippines, the land-grabbers are small farmers who are supported by the local authorities in their encroachments on tribal territory. Again, as in India, the political system is open enough to allow indigenous peoples to mobilize in their own defense, if they can, and to permit Non-Governmental Organizations (NGOs) and other sympathetic agencies to help them as they battle against the odds.

In Indonesia, until the fall of President Suharto in 1998, an authoritarian regime presided over a society that was officially and explicitly multiethnic. In that society, ethnic minorities were expected to retain their customary ways of life, provided they subscribed to the government's official philosophy of *Pancasila* (Five Principles): belief in a supreme God; humanitarianism; national unity; democracy; and social justice. The first of these principles is considered extremely important, with the result that doctrinal niceties are stretched to permit Hinduism and Buddhism to qualify along with Islam and Christianity. The Indonesian educational system encourages students to take pride in the religious and ethnic diversity of their country and to practice tolerance toward peoples of other faiths and other ethnicities. Tribal peoples seem, however, to strain the limits of this tolerance. Because tribal beliefs are considered "superstitions" rather than religions, the government encourages missionaries to work among tribal peoples and convert them to one of the major religions (usually Christianity).

It is in the most easterly region of Indonesia that tribal peoples have traditionally been most disadvantaged. This region, which the Indonesians call Irian Jaya, is part of the island of New Guinea and used to be part of the Dutch East Indies. Since Indonesia is the independent state that was formed out of the Dutch East Indies, it felt that Irian Jaya should rightfully be part of its post-colonial domain. It was not until 1963, however, that it succeeded in wresting control of Irian Jaya from the Dutch. Since then, reports from Irian Jaya indicate that Indonesia is adopting an internal colonialist stance toward the Irianese, whom they tend to regard as backward tribal peoples who must be civilized. For their part, the Irianese call themselves Papuans and their land West Papua. Many of them are unhappy with the treatment they receive from the Indonesians and a Free Papua Movement continues to fight a guerilla war against the occupying power.

The discontent of the Papuans is made worse by the fact that Irian Jaya is also a receiving area for transmigrants—people who are moved in government-sponsored programs from the densely (over)populated islands of Java, Madura, and Bali to the much more sparsely populated islands of Sumatra, Kalimantan (Borneo), Sulawesi, and now Irian Jaya. This has caused much unhappiness among the Papuans whose traditional uses of the land are being ignored and, therefore, go uncompensated as the government settles transmigrants on it. It seems clear that Indonesian insistence on settling transmigrants in Irian Jaya is not so much to solve problems of overpopulation in the central islands or to increase national levels of food production— explanations that have been officially abandoned—but rather to Javanize or at least de-Papuanize Irian Jaya. As Indonesia's foreign minister remarked in 1984, the influence of these more-advanced Indonesians can only be beneficial to the natives, who will be converted into farmers instead of continuing to be "nomads running around naked." Meanwhile, Papuan refugees continue to move from the Indonesian province into Papua New Guinea, the country across the border to the east.

A serious and long-standing accusation against Indonesia for the violation of group rights has to do with the Indonesian invasion of East Timor. East Timor, which was a Portuguese colony, was never part of the Dutch East Indies and did not wish to become part of Indonesia when the Dutch and the Portuguese withdrew. Indonesia invaded and occupied East Timor in 1975 because it would not tolerate, so close to home, what it considered to be the leftist politics of the East Timorese leaders. The invasion and the Indonesian army's slaughter of the East Timorese shocked the world at the time, but produced little but rhetorical support for the conquered islanders.

Sadly, the invasion and occupation of East Timor did not put an end to the suffering of its inhabitants. On the contrary, they were again brutalized after the fall of Suharto and the collapse of the interim presidency that succeeded him. When Abdurrahman Wahid took over the presidency, he permitted the East Timorese to vote on whether they wished to remain in Indonesia. Paramilitary forces closely related to the Indonesian army attempted to force the East Timorese to vote to stay in. When they voted to secede anyway, the paramilitaries went on the rampage, sacking communities, killing people, and forcing thousands to flee to refugee camps in West Timor. Eventually the United Nations stepped in and sent a force, largely composed of Australians, to protect the East Timorese from the government they had been trying to repudiate for decades. The East Timorese question is far from being resolved; it is one of the issues in eastern Indonesia that has more to do with power politics than with ethnicity or tribalism.

It is in mainland Southeast Asia that the relations between tribes and states are most complex. In that region especially the millennial interaction of states and rulers with dependent and marginal peoples were arbitrarily rearranged by the colonial powers in the nineteenth century and again by the wars that raged through the area in the twentieth and twenty-first centuries. For example, the Montagnards, who became famous in the world at large for their role during the war in Vietnam, traditionally maintained relationships with and paid tribute to the rulers in Laos and Cambodia. Under colonial and post-colonial rule, these traditional arrangements were cut off and the Montagnards became subjects of the Vietnamese state. Similarly the Karens were divided between Burma and Siam (later Thailand), and their cross-border relations with other polities and even among themselves were attenuated.

The troubled recent history of Burma (now renamed Myanmar by its present military rulers) shows the complex interplay of forces that have affected peoples in this part of the world.[13]

Burma was traditionally a meeting point of various civilizations. The Mon entered Burma from the east (Cambodia) in the sixth century BC, and since then the Arakanese established themselves in the west, the Burmans came from north and the Shan from the direction of China in the northeast. The region was an area of constant warfare between the Mon, Burmese, and Shan as they struggled to dominate each other. In the late nineteenth century, the British invaded from India and took Burma as a colony.

---

13. This discussion of the situation in Burma/Myanmar is taken from Mirante 1987.

The British governed the south-central area of Burma (with its large and mostly Burmese population) directly, modernizing its agriculture and encouraging the production of export crops. Traditional Burmese society decayed and the Burmese developed a deep animosity toward the British, which was demonstrated when the majority of them supported the Japanese as the latter were driving the British out of their Southeast Asian colonies during the second world war. The British had not administered the peoples along Burma's borders, such as the Karen and the Kachin, directly. They were administered as protectorates and largely left to run their own affairs. These peoples supported the British and fought the Japanese during the war.

After the war, Burma gained its independence from Britain, but securing internal peace and stability was more difficult. The border peoples hesitantly agreed to join the Federation of Burma, on the condition that their autonomy was respected and that they would have the right to withdraw from the Federation after ten years if they were not satisfied, but civil war soon broke out. Aung San, the father of Burmese independence, was assassinated by political rivals. Discrimination and killing of Christian Karens by the Buddhist majority inspired a Karen revolt. Soon communist, Arakanese, and Mon rebels were also fighting the government. Meanwhile, in the north, Chinese troops from Chiang Kai Shek's army, fleeing before the victorious communists in China's civil war, settled in the Shan state of northern Burma where they became important producers and shippers of opium for the international trade. Burmese conflict with these Chinese forces led to fighting with the Shan as well.

In 1962 General Ne Win, who had built up the Burmese army to deal with the many rebellions, staged a coup and took over the government of the country, which has remained in his hands ever since. Myanmar, as he renamed it, has been in a constant state of civil war, pitting the Burmese army against insurgents in all the border areas. The Karen rebels have been driven into the mountains along the Thai border and it is they that are most fiercely attacked by the Burmese army. There are also Mon, Karenni, Shan, Kachin, Naga, and Arakanese, as well as the descendents of the nationalist Chinese in the north, all fighting against the government.

Ne Win's regime has sought to isolate Myanmar from the rest of the world while it followed the "Burmese Way of Socialism." The economy has deteriorated, leaving Myanmar one of the poorest countries in the world, while the government and its rebel opponents trade in the commodities their regions control in order to finance their hostilities. Meanwhile, the Burmese army treats villagers in rebel areas with consistent brutality. They impose a pattern of forced labor, beatings, torture, and sexual abuse with the apparent intention of breaking the will to resist of the "uncivilized" tribal peoples whom they despise but have so far been unable to defeat.

Myanmar is thus a classic example of Southeast Asian complexity. It is a country where various civilizations meet. Its borders, arbitrarily set by a colonial power, inhibit contact between peoples who traditionally interacted with each other and mandate contact between peoples who have traditionally fought each other. The British administration sowed divisiveness between the Burmese and the other peoples of the country, divisions that were exacerbated during the second world war. Since then, the model of a federation, which might have enabled the peoples of the country to coexist peaceably in a single state, has been undermined, leading predictably to endless warfare.

Note that the question of which people or peoples are truly "indigenous" is not an issue in Myanmar. Furthermore the "tribalism" of the border peoples is equally elusive. The Shan near the northern border used to be ruled by princes whose subjects were settled peoples who themselves had and still have relations with "tribal" peoples at the margins of their territories. The Kachin used to be such a people, some of whom became Shan-ified, while others clung to their traditional Kachin ways. To this day the Pao-O, a Karen-speaking people living in the Shan state, retain their tribal ways, though they have considerable contact with their neighbors. The Karen themselves are a well-organized Christian group, with a population of more than three million. The "marginality" and "backwardness" attributed to these border peoples are not a result of their desire to maintain tribal ways, but rather expressions of Burmese prejudice.

AFRICA AND THE POLITICS OF TRIBALISM

There are certain peoples in Africa who are subjected to constant pressures and discrimination because they continue in their traditional, relatively isolated, and self-reliant ways of life. These are the nomadic pastoralists, peoples like the San and the !Kung (who used to be called Bushmen) and peoples like the Efe (who used to be called Pygmies). There are about 15 million pastoralists. In West Africa they live in the Sahel, a belt of semiarid land stretching all the way from Mauritania and Senegal to Chad, and lying between the Sahara desert to the north and the rich grasslands further south (see map on p. xiii). In East Africa they are found in Somalia and Ethiopia, the Sudan, Uganda, Kenya, and as far south as Tanzania. The prejudices against and pressures on nomadic pastoralists have already been discussed previously. Peoples like the San and the Efe are, by contrast, hunting and gathering peoples. There are perhaps 70,000 of the San and related peoples who inhabit the deserts of Southwest Africa, and about 200,000 of the Efe and related peoples in the rainforests of Central Africa, all of them set apart from the states in which they live by their traditional lifestyles.

Discussions of tribalism in Africa do not refer specifically to the backwardness of pastoralists or hunters and gatherers. The word in Africa has a quite different, although still negative, connotation. It is normally used to refer to a characteristic feature of African societies, and one that is regularly deplored, namely the tendency for people to identify primarily, if not exclusively, with their tribal group rather than with the state. So it is called "tribalism" if modern and sophisticated Ibo consider themselves Ibo rather than Nigerian, and the term in this context does not imply any backwardness on the part of the Ibo—except in so far as it may be considered backward not to identify with the state.

Tribalism is denounced throughout Africa as archaic. The state is held to represent modernity and those citizens who identify only with a part of it are considered parochial and pre-modern. Worse still, tribalism is considered a holdover from colonial days. When the Europeans reserved for themselves the right to be actors on the world stage, they kept Africans in their place by a policy of divide and rule. Europeans could have nations; Africans were confined to their tribes. Now that the African territories of the Europeans have become independent nations, so the argument runs, Africans should cease thinking in terms of their tribes. Some people would even go so far as to say that the tribes of Africa on the eve of independence were largely European creations, peoples who owed their very identities as well as their administrative existence to the manipulations of the colonial powers. This is an exaggeration. It is true that the colonial powers manipulated African tribes economically and politically and on occasion even determined their identities within the colonial state, as can be seen in the discussion of Rwanda in Chapter 3. Yet it is also true that the Africa that the colonialists conquered was a continent of distinct peoples who came to be known as tribes. The distinctions between them were real, though they could be emphasized and de-emphasized according to political convenience. These distinctions were a matter of ethnographic interest to the colonial authorities who did not expect the peoples of, say, Kenya to have much in common with each other apart from the fact that they were all subject to the British administration of the territory. The same distinctions do pose problems for the post-colonial states. Now disparate peoples, who may only share a common history of domination by a single colonial power, are expected to feel and act like members of the nation that unites them.

This has proved to be difficult, as the most eloquent spokespeople for African independence knew it would be. That is why they went out of their way to denounce tribalism. Kwame Nkrumah launched a campaign to do away with all mention of the tribes within Ghana. They were to be replaced by references to Ghana and Ghanaians (Hodgkin 1962). In francophone Africa, Sekou Touré took up a similar theme, insisting that in five years time (he was speaking in 1959), no one would remember the tribal entities of the old Africa (Touré 1959)! In those heady days, when the nations of Africa were still in the process of establishing their independence, African leaders spoke warmly of tribal traditions. For example, they praised the African (tribal) tradition of making decisions by consensus and made this into an argument for one-party states as being peculiarly appropriate in the African context. In fact, African leaders praised the qualities of tribal society and appealed to a kind of synthetic pan-African virtue based on these qualities, while at the same time attacking tribalism in its specific manifestations.

The weakness and instability of many African states is often attributed to the "tribalism" of their inhabitants, which is accordingly denounced by those who feel that modernization and progress depend on the strength of the state. Yet the tribalism that is so much criticized is more an effect of weak and corrupt states than its cause. African nations have agreed to maintain the colonial boundaries of their states. This is partly done to forestall endless boundary disputes throughout the continent, but it is also done to facilitate international recognition of the states in question. Because the capture of the state and the revenues, loans, and foreign aid that goes with it is the prime political prize in many parts of Africa, those competing for the state have a vested interest in ensuring that it is internationally recognized.

These "frozen" states therefore contain disparate peoples who lack the sense of a common history and a will to live together, which some writers have mentioned as being the essential characteristics of a nation (see Chapter 4). From this point of view, African tribalism refers simply to the tendency of individuals to identify with their people rather than with the state, which is considered an arbitrary conglomerate of disparate peoples. Moreover, these peoples, although they are referred to as "tribes" and the sentiments they inspire are referred to as "tribalism," are not usually tribes in the technical sense[14] but are in effect ethnic groups like those discussed in Chapter 2.

CONCLUSION

In this chapter we have seen that indigenous peoples are defined as much by their relations with the state as by any intrinsic characteris-

---

14. See the conclusion to this chapter.

tics that they may possess. They are often considered to be tribal peoples in the sense that they belong to small-scale preindustrial societies that live in comparative isolation and manage their own affairs without the centralized authority of a state. But we have also seen that the terms *tribal peoples* and *tribalism* are used much more broadly than that. Many peoples are stigmatized as "tribal," not because they fit the definition given above, but because they reject the authority of a state and do not wish to adopt the culture of the mainstream population that the state represents. They are in fact stigmatized as being "tribal" because they insist on being marginal.

Indigenous peoples are always marginal to their states and they are often tribal in the technical sense. Marginal peoples, though, as we saw from the Asian examples, are not necessarily either indigenous or tribal. They may be more like the ethnic groups and ethnic minorities to be discussed in Chapter 2. The point is that there are no hard and fast distinctions that enable us to place societies unambiguously within these categories. Instead, we are dealing with a continuum that ranges from *indigenous/tribal* peoples to *indigenous* (but not tribal) peoples, to peoples *stigmatized as tribal,* to peoples considered *ethnic minorities* to peoples considered *nationalities,* though they coexist in a single state.

This last usage was employed in the former Soviet Union and still is in the People's Republic of China. In China it is clear that not all nationalities are equivalent. The Han Chinese nationality is dominant, both culturally and numerically within the state. Other nationalities are minorities. Indeed, they are sometimes referred to in English as *national minorities,* which is also the official term used in the Philippines for all their minorities—indigenous, tribal, or otherwise. Chinese national minorities resemble indigenous peoples in that they tend to be marginal to the state, which in its turn makes sporadic efforts to assimilate them both politically and culturally. In most other ways, however, they are more like ethnic minorities and so they will be discussed in the next chapter.

There is another way in which the concept of *tribalism* is much in use nowadays—when it refers to the tendency for people of the same ethnicity to band together in modern societies. There has been much discussion in the world's press about the dire effects of tribalism in Europe and serious writers in the United States have urged Americans not to be lured down the slippery slope of multiculturalism into their own kind of tribalism. This kind of tribalism is usually thought to be the consequence of an innate tendency among human beings to band together with their own kind and fight all those that are different. I mention it here just to complete the discussion of the various uses of the term *tribalism.* I shall discuss it more fully when I deal with the state in Chapter 4.

In spite of all these definitional difficulties, the indigenous peoples who are the focus of this chapter have a sufficiently clear sense of themselves, their problems, and their place in the world to have finally succeeded in getting their issues onto the agenda of the United Nations. A Working Group on Indigenous Rights has been meeting under the auspices of the United Nations and has issued a draft declaration on what those rights should be. Some of the terms of that declaration, which I cite below, are instructive. The indigenous peoples ask for: 1) self-determination within existing states, 2) protection against genocide, 3) protection against ethnocide, 4) protection of their own cultures, 5) protection of their own institutions of governance, 6) protection of their own special relationship to the land, 7) protection of their traditional economic activities, and 8) representation on all bodies making decisions about them.

The declaration makes it clear once and for all that secession and separatism are not on the mainstream agenda of indigenous peoples. What they want is a recognition of their rights within existing states, but the rights they want recognized are far reaching. To ask not to be massacred (protection against genocide) is hardly remarkable. All peoples should have such a right. It is only significant that indigenous peoples should feel that they need specifically to ask for it and to have it guaranteed. The other rights demanded are cultural, political, and economic. Indigenous peoples ask that they be allowed to maintain their own traditions, their own ways of governing themselves, and their own ways of making a living off the land. They also ask that they have a chance to ensure that these rights are respected by being represented on all bodies that make decisions about them. These requests, if granted, would entail a rethinking and reorganization of most states in the world, as well as a rethinking of the ways in which economic activities are organized within them. The indigenous charter thus poses a direct challenge to the state as we have come to know it, and that challenge will be discussed in Chapter 4.

2

Ethnic Groups

UNCERTAIN ETHNICITY

Ethnicity has a will-o'-the-wisp quality that makes it extremely hard to analyze and not much easier to discuss. Everyone knows that it is a kind of fellow-feeling that binds people together and makes them feel distinct from others, yet it is difficult to say precisely what kind of feeling it is and why and when people will be strongly affected by it. Some people under some circumstances are willing to die and certainly to kill on behalf of their ethnic group. Other people under other circumstances are hardly aware of their own ethnicity and pay it little attention in their everyday lives. So what is ethnicity and why does it have this evanescent quality?

Ethnicity is like kinship. When people recognize each other as belonging to the same ethnic group, they feel like distant kin, vaguely related to each other through common descent, but so far back that no one can trace the precise relationship. The ethnicity of such a group is its members' idea of their own distinctiveness from others. It is invariably based on a sense of common history, usually combined with other characteristics, such as sharing the same race, religion, language, or culture. Some groups may have a common ethnicity imputed to them, without feeling or recognizing it themselves. A classic example is the "Indians" of the Americas, a diverse series of distinct populations that were frequently lumped together by newcomers to the hemisphere. Ethnicity is thus a sense of relatedness that is ascribed to peoples, either by themselves or by others or both. It also resembles kinship in another way, namely that ethnic groups, like kin groups, may or may not have a strong sense of identity, and they may or may not stick together.

Yet there is one important difference between family ties and ethnic ties. Everybody everywhere normally starts life as the member of a family and must at some time or another act as one. This is true even in societies that try to curtail the functions of the family, as the former Soviet Union once did, or in societies where families seem reduced to vanishing point, as in some parts of the United States. Family ties, however defined, could be said in this sense to be truly primordial links. This is not so of ethnic ties. Everyone has a latent qualification for ethnic association, in that we all speak a language, have a skin color, live in places that have a history, and so on, but these (or other) criteria do not necessarily make us members of ethnic groups. Ethnicity only comes into play when one or more of these criteria are activated and said to be the defining characteristics of a group. That is why the manipulation of ethnicity plays such an important part in discussions of the topic.

The criteria for distinguishing ethnic groups from each other represent a selection and interpretation of the "facts" pertaining to them. Religion may serve to distinguish an ethnic group in some places and be an unmarked criterion in others. Ethnicity may depend on skin color in some places and not in others. A common language may distinguish an ethnic group or may not. French-speakers as such do not, for example, constitute an ethnic group, yet being French-speaking in Quebec is the most important criterion for distinguishing a self-conscious ethnic group that wishes to turn Quebec into an independent country. Similarly, language is the most important criterion for distinguishing the major ethnic groups of Belgium (the French-speaking Walloons and the Dutch-speaking Flemings) from each other. Perhaps the most sensitive and malleable criterion is the sense of common history. Ethnic groups must have a shared sense of their past, but that past, as I mentioned in the preface, is open to construction or reinterpretation in a variety of ways that may have tragic consequences in the present.

It is, therefore, vitally important to understand the histories that lead up to and permeate ethnic conflicts. In the following chapters, I do not have the space to analyze varying perceptions of history as one ideally should. I try instead to give as fair a presentation as I can of the histories of the interethnic situations I discuss. These are, of course, my interpretations, derived from the data presented by the specialists whom I cite. Their purpose is to give the reader a clear understanding of situations that are sometimes so complex that reasonable people could be excused for throwing up their hands and banishing them to that mental trash can that we call "tribal conflict."

Ethnic groups do not form because people are of the same race or share the same language or the same culture. They form because people who share such characteristics *decide* they are members of a distinct group, or because people who share such characteristics are *lumped together* and treated by outsiders as members of a distinct group. As Fredrik Barth pointed out long ago (1969), it is not the common culture of a group that leads them to think of themselves as ethnically related, but the other way round. Once people are considered to be ethnically related, they establish rules and understandings concerning the essence and limits of what they have in common and who belongs and who does not.

These mechanisms for maintaining the boundaries of the group are critically important, for it is they that enable the group to persist. People must know whether others can be admitted to the group, whether it is possible to "pass" as one of the group, either formally or informally. They also need to know how far an individual can deviate from the norms and behaviors of the group before he or she will be no longer considered a member of it. Above all, they need to know how much and what kinds of interactions members of the group may have with outsiders if the group is to retain its identity.

Ethnic groups are never isolates. They invariably have contact with others and their members invariably interact with each other across group boundaries, even where there is hostility between groups. That is why understandings about boundaries and their maintenance are absolutely critical; the stronger the ethnic sentiment that binds a group together, the more strictly will its members try to enforce the boundaries, which explains why interethnic marriages often meet resistance from the families concerned. In fact, the way such marriages are regarded—unthinkable, to be discouraged, of no consequence, or encouraged—says a great deal about people's ideas concerning their own ethnicity and the interethnic situation in which they find themselves.

In the following chapters, I shall focus on ethnic groups and the conflicts between them, not so much on what ethnicity means to individuals caught up in those situations or how it affects the personal strategies that they develop in order to live their lives. I adopt an institutional approach that looks at how ethnic groups come to be defined with respect to each other, and also at the triangular relationship between ethnic groups, other ethnic groups, and the state.

Clearly there is an overlap between peoples and situations dealt with in the previous chapter and those treated in this one. This is consistent with my argument that indigenous peoples and ethnic groups are part of a continuum. All indigenous peoples are ethnic groups (or at least ethnic categories, if ethnicity is ascribed to people who have no sense of themselves as a group), but not all ethnic groups are indigenous. We are dealing here with a continuum that runs from small, marginal societies to larger, less marginal ones, to substatal societies that may even be referred to as nationalities or nations.

Most polities in the course of human history (other than isolated, tribal societies) have been multiethnic and multicultural, often with one ethnic group dominating the others. The idea, that the polity should be the state and that the state should correspond to a single culture (perhaps even be the preserve of a single people) is a relatively recent one. After the first world war, when President Wilson presented his fourteen points as a basis for maintaining peace in Europe (and hence, as it was then thought, throughout the world), his plan called for *self-determination* as the criterion for tracing the boundaries of states. Many of the peoples who would determine their own futures in this way had not had their own states before the war and, in some cases, had never had their own states. They were what we would nowadays call ethnic groups. Such a group is potentially a state, especially if it is large enough and occupies a contiguous area. Wilson was in effect proposing that such groups ought in principle to have the right to become independent states. This could, of course, only be done where it was politically feasible. In Europe after the first world war, that meant largely in the former Austro-Hungarian Empire that, as one of the losers in the war, was being dismembered by the victors.

Strangely enough, the terms *ethnicity* and *ethnic group* only came into use recently. They began to be used systematically around the 1950s. By then it was becoming clear that the frequent conflicts between substatal groups all over the world necessitated the use of a term that referred to people who felt bound together by ties that were somewhere between kinship and nationality—all the more so because such ties were not evaporating, as it had been supposed they would in the course of modernization. In fact, in many of the more "modern" nations of North America and Western Europe, such as Canada, Spain, France, Belgium, and the United Kingdom, ethnicity was growing stronger or re-emerging rather than disappearing. It became clear, in short, that ethnic attachments and the groups created by them were not obsolescent. They were an enduring social form that merited more analysis than they had previously received.

With the intensification of ethnic conflicts around the world in recent decades and particularly since the breakup of the former Soviet Union and the end of the cold war, it is difficult to remember that (and even more so—why) ethnicity remained comparatively ignored for so long. A tentative answer to that question will be given in Chapter 4, where I discuss the theoretical fixation of much Western writing on the desirability—and inevitability—of the liberal state. We now appear to have gone to the other extreme. Ethnicity is getting all too much attention and is normally linked with the idea of conflict. Yet it is a historical fact that peoples who considered themselves ethnically distinct from each other have often lived side by side or even intertwined with each other for long periods of time without serious conflict. This chapter will therefore analyze interethnic situations in various parts of the world in order to gain a better understanding not only of ethnic conflict but also of ethnic coexistence.

The chapter deals with states that are explicitly multiethnic. There are not as many of these as one might suppose, because governments and theorists have both tended to consider that the encouragement, even the toleration of multiethnicity is a recipe for disaster. I deal first with the two large multiethnic states that until recently occupied the greater part of the Eurasian land mass, the former Soviet Union, and the People's Republic of China, in order to examine how a vast array of peoples have related (and been required to relate) to each other in a part of the world where different ethnic groups, peoples, and nationalities have been interacting with each other for millennia.

I then look at two other modern states, Indonesia and Spain, who are trying with varied success (and in quite different ways) to defuse potential ethnic conflict by permitting ethnic differences to be expressed within their respective systems.

LARGE MULTIETHNIC STATES

The Former Soviet Union[1]

The Soviet Union was the successor to one of the last great land empires created by Europeans during the age of their expansion. The Austro-Hungarian empire was dismantled after the first world war. The overseas empires of the other European powers disintegrated after the second world war. The only continuity with the old imperial regimes was, curiously enough, in two dramatically different regions of the world—in the Americas and in the Soviet Union. In the Americas, the original imperialists proclaimed themselves to be natives and severed their formal ties with Europe, thus giving a new lease on life to the postimperial order. In the Soviet Union, the communist regime inherited, expanded, and continued to control the old Tsarist empire.

Since the middle ages the Russians had been extending their control outward from Moscow. At the end of the reign of Catherine the Great (1796), the western boundary of the empire ran through what is Poland today (see map inside back cover). It included what are now the Baltic states and much of the Caucasus and extended eastward as far as the Ural mountains. The nineteenth century saw a huge territorial expansion that included Central Asia and Siberia. The Tsarist empire at the beginning of the twentieth century, therefore, embraced not only a vast land mass but also a variety of peoples, some large and some small, speaking a bewildering array of languages. Under

---

1. The materials in this section are drawn especially from Barfield 1994, Fondahl 1992, Szpörluk 1990, Tishkov 1994, and Yamskov 1994.

the Tsarist autocracy, these peoples were expected to demonstrate loyalty to the Tsar, who was by God's will the sole power and head of the church. He was the Emperor of the Russias, of the *Russiskaia Imperiia*, and they owed allegiance to him personally. They were not technically subject to the Russians, for this was not a Russian Empire, which would have been called a *Russkaia Imperiia* (Szpörluk 1990: 2). In this way, the Tsars theoretically avoided the question of the precise relationship (or hierarchy of relationships) between the peoples of the empire. In practice, of course, it may have been an empire of all the Russias, but it was controlled by a Russian Tsar and the Russians had pride of place in it.

After the Russian revolution, as the Bolsheviks consolidated their control over the empire, they realized that the nationalities question posed a problem for them. Lenin's intention was to centralize power in the hands of the communist party and, through the party, to forge absolute unity within the Soviet state, but he realized that this would be difficult to do in an age of nationalism. The subject peoples of the Ottoman and Austro-Hungarian empires had broken free of their imperial masters. How would the Bolsheviks prevent a similar trend in the empire they had taken over? Lenin's solution was to put forward a constitution according to which the Russians would be only one of a number of equal peoples within the Soviet state. They would perhaps be the first among equals, but constitutionally the peoples of the Soviet Union would indeed be equals in a multiethnic confederation.

This was a truly revolutionary idea, further developed by Stalin who was the party theorist on the nationalities question. He organized the Soviet Union along ethnic or rather (in Soviet terms) along national lines. This did not mean, even in theory, that each distinct peoples of the Soviet Union could be granted their own territory and some degree of autonomy, for there were too many peoples (and some of them with very small populations) for this to be practicable. Instead he organized the Soviet state in an administrative hierarchy. At the apex were the Soviet Socialist Republics, which could in theory coin their own money, establish their own ties with foreign countries, and even secede from the Union. There were originally twelve of these, including the Russian Republic itself, but the number was increased to fifteen after the Soviet Union seized control of Estonia, Latvia, and Lithuania during the second world war. These republics were each conceptually the domain of their titular ethnic groups (or nationalities, as they were called in the Soviet Union), but they were also multiethnic.

Within the Soviet Socialist Republics there were Autonomous Republics, also defined in terms of a titular nationality. These in turn contained Autonomous Provinces, and Autonomous Districts and National Regions, on the lowest rung of the hierarchy. The whole administrative structure implied a great deal of autonomy throughout, associated (except at the very lowest levels) with the nationalities or peoples of the Soviet Union. This would have a double advantage. It would defuse the nationalist threat to the union by allowing the expression of ethnicity within the system. At the same time it would only need to do this temporarily because, according to orthodox Marxist theory, ethnicity and nationalism were part of the false consciousness of people who were still in the bourgeois, presocialist stage of human development. Once they understood that history was determined by class struggle and understood their own place in that struggle, they would see things in terms of class rather than ethnicity, which would gradually fade away. In the meantime the soviet state would have to see to it that its institutionalization of ethnicity was not allowed to impede progress toward the triumph of socialism,[2] when ethnic attachments would disappear because they had no further relevance.

In fact, the practice never remotely matched the theory. The Soviet Socialist Republics were strictly controlled from Moscow and allowed to exercise none of the rights that were theoretically theirs.[3] Stalin decided which peoples of the USSR were to receive formal recognition and what this would entail. It is estimated that there are anywhere between 300 and 800 distinct ethnic groups in the former Soviet Union[4] but only about 100 were formally recognized (Fondahl 1992: 24–25). There were only fifteen Autonomous Republics, including the three Baltic states that were annexed during the second world war, each named for its titular nationality such as Russian, Estonian, Georgian, Uzbek, and so on (see map inside front cover). This meant that each republic contained a mosaic of ethnic groups other than the one it was named for. Furthermore, the members of titular nationalities could and did live outside "their own" republics, with the result that the former Soviet Union contained a remarkable mixture of different peoples, both recognized and unrecognized.

Recognition, in Stalin's time, did not entail autonomy for the peoples concerned, but it did bring other important benefits. Peoples so recognized had the right to use their own languages and to publish

---

2. The communist party in the Soviet Union always insisted that it was building "socialism" so I use the term here to avoid confusion. Democratic socialists would insist, however, that Soviet policy represented a Stalinist perversion of true socialism, which was never seriously attempted in the USSR.
3. Though Stalin did manage to obtain seats and votes for Belarus and Ukraine as well as the USSR in the United Nations. Those negotiations are discussed in Chapter 3.
4. No precise listing is available.

books, magazines, and newspapers in them. The Soviet Union subsidized an elaborate network of translators and printing houses to help bring out these materials and demonstrate the multiethnicity of the system. Recognized peoples could also maintain their religions, though this was a limited right, given the aggressive atheism of the Soviet state. They were likewise entitled to be represented by their own political leaders. This meant that Moscow approved local leaders, who then went to Moscow and returned to carry out Moscow's policies in their own "autonomous" republics or regions. None of these rights were granted to unrecognized ethnic groups. They were given neither the permission nor the means to maintain their own languages, cultures, and institutions and struggled as best they could against the full force of Soviet assimilationism.

Nor was that the worst that could happen to them. Some peoples were singled out for especially harsh treatment. For example, the Crimean Tatars[5] (Payin 1992a) and the Meshtikhetian Turks[6] (Payin 1992b) were uprooted from their homes and transplanted, at a moment's notice, to distant regions of the USSR. These population transfers targeted peoples whom Stalin had decided were security risks during the second world war and the transfers were carried out with dreadful brutality. Families were separated, often forever. In the case of the Crimean Tatars, the women and children of men fighting in the Soviet forces against the Germans were simply removed from their homes and sent away, without their husbands' even knowing where they had been taken to. Hundreds of thousands of people died in these removals, which were intended to annihilate the peoples concerned as distinct ethnic groups. A similar fate overtook the Kurds. In the 1920s a Kurdish National District had been formed in Azerbaidzhan, where Kurdish newspapers were published and education was in the Kurdish language, but Stalin put a stop to that in the 1930s. The Kurdish district was abolished. Kurds lost their recognition and eventually were forcibly deported from their homeland and scattered over no less than nine different republics (Nadirov 1992).

In fact, the Stalinist policy toward nationalities within the Soviet Union manipulated their lands and their ethnicity while claiming all the while to be guaranteeing their autonomy. The creation of the Jewish Autonomous Territory is a case in point (Wixman 1992: 22). In the 1930s, Zionists were demanding that the Soviet Union either give Soviet Jews their own territory or allow them to emigrate. So, in 1934

---

5. These people have lived since the fifteenth century in the Crimea, which became, under Stalin, part of the Ukrainian SSR.
6. These people have lived in Georgia since at least the sixteenth century.

Stalin created an Autonomous Territory for Soviet Jews, which allowed him to project an image of ethnic benevolence, for where else in the world were Jews so favored? In fact, the Territory was located in the unprepossessing far eastern reaches of Siberia around the remote city of Birobidzhan. Only a few optimistic Jews ever went there, but it enabled Stalin to tell Jews within the Soviet Union that if they wanted special rights for Jews, they must enjoy them in their own territory, just as Ukrainians did in the Ukraine and so on.

Ethnic groups were not only subject to deportation or virtual exile, as with the Jews, but they could also have their boundaries manipulated in order to separate groups who had thought of themselves as one people. For example, the Kirghiz were a people with three different kinds of ecological adaptation. Some of them were nomads on the steppes, some of them were transhuman nomads who traveled between fixed places, and some of them settled for part of the year along the shores of the Aral Sea. Stalin divided them along these lines and gave each group a separate territory—Kirghizia, Kazakhstan, and Karakalpakia. Having created the ethnic territories, he then sponsored the introduction of three separate literary languages to confirm his insistence that these were three distinct peoples (Wixman 1992: 22).

Alternatively, as we have seen, whole populations were transferred to create ethnic enclaves in regions dominated by another ethnicity. The consequences of these policies became tragically apparent when Gorbachev initiated his policy of glasnost, the gradual loosening of central control within the Soviet Union. On the one hand, the ethnic rhetoric of Stalinist times and the maintenance of ethnically defined boundaries as well as the support of what the Soviets considered the facade of ethnicity—languages, customs, folk dances, and so on—served to keep ethnic consciousness alive in the Soviet Union. It showed, however, little sign of disappearing, as it was supposed to, when New Soviet Man replaced his ethnically inclined ancestors. On the other hand, Stalinist brutalities, preferences for some peoples over others, and manipulations of ethnic boundaries left behind a bitter legacy. The maps were scrambled, so that the quest for self-determination in the post-Stalinist era is even more difficult than it might otherwise have been. Translocated peoples wish to return to their old lands, which brings them into conflict with those who have taken them over. Others fight to rectify or maintain the boundaries established during Stalin's time. In yet other places there are hierarchies of claims to lands and resources giving rise to what has been called the problem of "Matrioshka nationalism," referring to the Russian dolls that nest in series, each one containing a smaller one (Fondahl 1992: 20).

The worst aspect of the legacy of Stalinism is his territorializing of ethnicity. The Soviet Union was, of course, multiethnic, but each of its republics was defined in ethnic terms. This meant that each contained a titular people or nationality, and also meant that each contained a number of nationalities that theoretically had no rights there. This was not particularly important when all these rights were fictitious anyway and the whole union was run despotically from Moscow, but it became critically important after the collapse of the Soviet Union. The former republics then emerged as independent states with, as often as not, little commitment to multiethnicity. Although the Soviet Union still existed, it did not much matter if, say, a Ukrainian lived and worked in Georgia. Once it ceased to exist, that same Ukrainian was now a foreigner in a newly independent state where he had no special rights. Not only did people who had never considered themselves minorities suddenly find themselves classed as such, but people who *had* considered themselves minorities also discovered that they had even smaller minorities (the "double minorities") in their midst and that these too were clamoring for self-determination. The situation of the large Russian populations, now minorities, in the newly independent states, which they had thought were mere subdivisions of the Soviet Union, is a particularly delicate issue. Many of these people made their homes outside the Russian Republic, but they continued to speak Russian in a Russian-dominated Soviet Union. Now they find themselves considered minorities, and often resented for their previous domination and their failure to learn the language of the place where they live. It is very difficult for such people to return to Russia, which is in economic crisis. Meanwhile, Russian nationalists are stridently insisting that their countrymen in what they call the "Near Abroad" should not be abandoned. The problem is reminiscent of the crisis that rocked France concerning the future of the large number of French settlers in Algeria, except that Russia now faces a dozen "Algerian" crises all around its new borders.

During this ethnic turmoil, the indigenous peoples of the former Soviet Union are in grave danger of being forgotten and pushed aside. When the Soviet Union still existed, it contained (seen through Russian eyes) a kind of hierarchy of peoples. At the top stood the Russians, elder brothers to all the rest and particularly close to their fellow Slavs from Ukraine and Belarus. They regarded themselves as a cut above the other Europeans within the union—the Baltic peoples, Greeks, Moldavians, and peoples from the Caucasus. These people in turn felt themselves somewhat superior to the large nationalities of Asiatic origin, who for their part looked down on those whom we might call the "indigenous peoples" (Kaapcke 1992).

These latter peoples are denominated by a Russian phrase meaning, literally, the "small-in-number peoples of the North." The name was given to them when the designation referred largely to migratory herders or people who lived by hunting and gathering in Siberia and the far north, and was retained for small, marginal societies in other parts of the Soviet Union, even the far south. Such peoples did not qualify for their own pieces of independent territory because they did not satisfy two of Stalin's three requirements for self-determination. These were: economic self-sufficiency, which they possessed, but also sufficient numbers and a developed civilization, both of which they were felt to lack. Consequently, they have been treated much like indigenous peoples in other countries—lacking clearly defined rights to land or self-determination and administered directly by a state that expected them to vanish as separate peoples in the not too distant future.

The supreme irony of the Soviet nationalities policy is that it was calculated to manipulate and neutralize ethnicity (until such time as it evaporated) to prevent it undermining the state. But ethnicity did not evaporate in the Soviet Union any more than it has done elsewhere. Meanwhile Soviet policy gave it a kind of legitimacy, which may not have been taken seriously by Stalin, but is taken with the utmost seriousness in the post-Soviet republics.

These countries find themselves in a difficult situation. They are, together with Russia itself, passing through a period of traumatic uncertainty. The former Soviet Union has collapsed and with it all the rigid institutions that previously structured the lives of its inhabitants. These have suddenly discovered that they are not citizens of a great power, but inhabitants of relatively poor and in some cases relatively insignificant countries. In fact, many of them discovered that they inhabited countries of which they never expected and did not want to be citizens. Even these countries had little stability, as groups within them attempted to secede, or as groups outside of them claimed territory that lay within them. In this time of economic and political uncertainty, the inhabitants of post-Soviet states had few institutions to fall back on. The Soviet regime had been despotic, intrusive, and all regulatory. Its disappearance left a void. Its citizens, uncertain of their place in the world, of their nationality, or how they would make ends meet, had weak informal networks or nongovernmental associations to sustain them.

It is in such circumstances that people are constrained to band together with others of their own kind and ethnic chauvinism comes to the fore. This is especially the case in post-Soviet states, which were ethnically defined in the first place, are ethnically thoroughly mixed, and where the collapse of the Soviet Union has led to a great ethnic sorting out. Soviet (and particularly Stalin's) policies stressed the principle that peoples were entitled to their own territories. They then moved peoples around and gerrymandered territories to produce an ethnic jigsaw puzzle infinitely more convoluted than would have been produced by the normal flow of people within the Soviet economy. This left a potentially explosive situation for post-soviet states to deal with.

Boris Yeltsin argued for multiethnic solutions (see Tishkov 1994: 54) but most other leaders did not see it that way. The majority of leaders in the post-soviet era are old communists who have clung to power by reinventing themselves as spokespeople for the nationalisms of their own peoples. They have become the new ethnic entrepreneurs, or manipulators of ethnicity—Stalin was the old one. Valery Tishkov, who used to be Minister for Minorities in Moscow and therefore has considerable experience in these matters, writes that "in recent years practically all major political careers (in the Former Soviet Union) as well as state politics and projects are shaping around ethnic or nationalistic appeals and manipulations" (Tishkov 1994: 54). These new political careerists have, however, had the benefit of the old and not yet superannuated system, in which leaders were powerful, unaccountable, and in control of the media. This is particularly important since, as Tishkov points out, most people are not eager to do battle against other ethnic groups. They must be psychologically prepared, or one might say "worked up" for it and this is exactly what they were in country after country of the former Soviet Union. This leads Tishkov to raise the difficult topic of how to control hate speech, to which I shall return later. In the meantime, this volatile situation was ripe for ethnic cleansing, at least in the sense of expelling peoples considered somehow "out of place" in territories now controlled by others, and there was indeed a wave of such actions in the years immediately following the collapse of the Soviet Union.

This outline of the nationalities policy of the former Soviet Union shows that the ethnic conflicts now taking place in that part of the world are the result of the political manipulations of ethnicity, first in the Stalinist period and next in the period when the Soviet Union was breaking up. This becomes even clearer if we look at what has happened in (once-Soviet) Central Asia.

Central Asia[7]

Central Asia is a huge landlocked region that for two thousand years has lain astride the "Silk Route" linking East and West. It was constantly invaded by nomadic conquerors who would eventually settle down and blend in with the local inhabitants. By the seventeenth century, the three major hubs of the region, ruled by their own khans,

---

7. The material in this section is taken primarily from Barfield 1994.

were centered on the cities of Bukhara, Khiva, and Kokand. The settled populations of these Khanates occupied the irrigated river valleys and the cities. They were a mixture of long-settled Iranians and newly arrived Turkic peoples who intermarried, shared a common culture, and were bilingual in Persian and Uzbek. In the outlying regions, away from the cities and intensive agriculture, dwelt peoples who were loosely tied to or sometimes quite independent of the Khanates. There were Uzbeks in the hills and Persian-speaking Tajiks in the mountains. There were Kazakh pastoral nomads in the vast steppes of the north, Turkmen wandering in the deserts to the southwest and Kirghiz using the mountain pastures in the Pamir mountains. There were also smaller minority peoples who were recognized as distinct—Arabs, Tatars, old Jewish communities in Samarkand and Bukhara, and Ismaili Muslims in the Pamirs speaking ancient Iranian languages that had died out everywhere else (Barfield 1994: 48).

In this mixture of peoples and languages, political and economic relationships came to be more important than ethnic ones. The Turkic nomads who had conquered the area needed Persian-speaking assistants to help them administer the Khanates, which gave rise to the old Central Asian proverb: "A Turk without a Tajik is like a head without a hat." In this truly multiethnic region the peoples of the cities lived intermingled, some conscious of their own ethnic identities, others less so. Away from the cities, the various peoples of Central Asia exploited different ecological niches and thus had symbiotic and peaceful relations with each other. The only ones who maintained a strong and exclusive sense of tribal identity were the most peripheral nomads.

All this began to change with the imposition of Tsarist rule in the 1870s. The Russians introduced intensive cotton growing into the region and took over the lands of many pastoral nomads, whose way of life they deemed "irrational." Greater changes came in 1920 when Central Asia became part of the Soviet Union. Peoples who had long been accustomed to maintaining contacts in all directions along traditional trade routes were now cut off from their eastern connections and reoriented toward Moscow. The Khanates of Khiva and Bukhara, which had continued to exist as Russian protectorates under the Tsars, were dismantled and replaced by the five Autonomous Republics of Kazakhstan, Uzbekistan, Turkmenistan, Tajikistan, and Kirghizstan. These autonomous republics, in keeping with the Stalinist theory already discussed, were supposed, as their names imply, to be the territories of particular peoples, but in fact Central Asia had never been organized that way. People derived their identity from a common regional culture sharing the Islamic faith, using Persian or one of the Turkic languages, writing them in Arabic script, and so on.

For these reasons, there were those who called for the peoples of Central Asia to unite in a "Greater Turkestan," but they were suppressed. Instead, the Soviet Union took care to divide the Central Asians into competing groups that in theory possessed distinct languages, cultures, and histories. The ethnic identity of individuals thus became important for the first time. It made a difference whether a person was of the titular nationality in a republic or not and, if not, what nationality he or she declared. But declaring a nationality was not so easy. It was a relatively simple matter for nomadic Turkmen or Kirghiz but much harder for the mixed sedentary populations. Should individuals who spoke both languages and lived in a mixed culture declare themselves Tajik or Uzbek? How about the smaller groups who thought of themselves, for example, as Uighurs or Tatars? Some of these simply amalgamated with larger groups for administrative convenience. Members of the same family might opt for different nationalities based on personal preference or the advantages they perceived as attaching to their choice.

The boundaries of the new ethnic republics were, of course, arbitrary. In most places the populations were so mixed it was impossible to draw a line that separated ethnic groups from one another. When the boundaries were drawn, they had the effect of lumping together communities and regions that had had no previous connection and, worse still, splitting up those that had. This created disputes over land and resources because it interfered with use patterns that had taken centuries to develop. As Barfield puts it (1994: 49): "Soviet policy had ripped a vibrant human tapestry into pieces and then attempted to sort the resulting threads by their primary colors."

During the Soviet era, the disputes arising from the administrative carve-up of Central Asia were muted. Peoples still traveled relatively easily from one republic to another and policy was set in Moscow anyway, so regional leaders could not be held responsible for the vagaries of economic planning and resource use. When the Soviet Union broke up, the situation changed. The boundaries between the Autonomous Republics of Soviet Central Asia suddenly became international frontiers. The leaders of these republics, party functionaries who had previously been responsible for putting Mosow's policies into effect, now found themselves heads of state. As such, they were required to make decisions with both national and international consequences. Their republics suddenly became the official homelands of their dominant nationalities, and the leaders had to decide what the relationship of the dominant nationalities should be to the other peoples in their new states as well as to the substantial Russian populations that lived in them and were quite unaccustomed to thinking of themselves as minorities.

The result was a series of conflicts in Central Asia that appear to be ethnically motivated. This seems most apparent in Kazakhstan, the largest of the Central Asian republics and the one with the second largest population, after Uzbekistan. The Kazakhs are actually in a minority in their own republic, being slightly outnumbered by the combined total of Russians and Ukrainians living there. The Slavs dominate wheat cultivation and industry in Kazakhstan's diversified and comparatively wealthy economy. Meanwhile, the Kazakhs resent the patronizing attitude of the Westerners who let it be known that they have been "civilizing" the backward natives. Kazakhs are now in competition with Slavs over land rights and jobs, but the government of the republic has to proceed with care. It cannot seem to be too hard on the Slavic majority, for Kazakhstan has a long frontier with Russia and used to be considered the strategic heart of the former Soviet Union.[8] Russian nationalists have already expressed their displeasure that such a territory, with its large population of Slavs, should have been allowed to become part of the "Near Abroad," and they are certain to demand action if they feel that their brother Slavs are not being treated right in Kazakhstan. The Kazakh government thus faces the extraordinarily difficult task of trying to create a Kazakh identity in its republic without alienating the Slavic majority (Barfield 1994: 50).

Uzbekistan is in a very different situation. It is the most populous of all the Central Asian republics and Uzbeks make up more than 70 percent of its population. It has inherited the three great regional cities of Tashkent, Bukhara, and Samarkand and most of the key agricultural areas of the old Khanates, together with massive Soviet-inspired cotton production. It was, therefore, confident enough to move without delay to insist that Uzbek be the official language of the republic. This gave extra impetus to the Russian exodus from Uzbekistan, because it is a republic in which they see no future for themselves.

Turkmenistan, with a small and homogenous population, used to be considered one of the most economically backward regions of the former Soviet Union, but it is now in the fortunate position of knowing that it possesses large deposits of oil and natural gas that will certainly make it extremely wealthy.

Kirghizstan lies in a mountainous region of such beauty that the republic hopes to encourage a tourist trade in the near future. Meanwhile,

---

8. Not only because of the wealth of its resources. The vast expanses of Kazakhstan also led the former Soviet Union to use it for testing and siting its atomic weapons.

there have been clashes between Kirghiz and Uzbeks over land rights because the Uzbeks control the best agricultural land.

It is Tajikistan, however, that is generally regarded as the most troubled republic in the region. It is an impoverished republic created for Tajiks, who originally occupied a mountainous hinterland that was connected to the major cities of Central Asia. Now cut off from those cities, Tajikistan is a hinterland with no metropolitan center. As a result, its relations with Uzbekistan have been troubled by arguments over the legitimacy of borders, over the status of Uzbeks in Tajikistan, and vice versa. A glance at the map shows how curiously the borders are constructed in this region, with a mountainous spur of Tajikistan penetrating Uzbekistan and almost cutting off Kokand and its rich agricultural land, which remain in eastern Uzbekistan. Similarly Samarkand, further south, which had a large Tajik population, was left in Uzbekistan, just outside the borders of Tajikistan.

It is in Tajikistan that the worst conflicts in the region have occurred. The civil war in that republic was seen by the Russians, who sent troops to keep the Tajik government in power, as a battle against Islamic fundamentalists, who were accused of fanning local ethnic tensions. The explanation was easily accepted in the west, which considers that ethnic tensions are rife in Central Asia (and in most other places too) and is extremely sensitive about Islamic fundamentalism. In fact the civil war was occasioned by the anger of much of the population over the disastrous economic situation in the republic and the responsibility of the old communists (now turned new republican leaders) for poverty, inefficiency, and the suppression of Central Asian culture.[9] Schoeberlein-Engel argues that the causes of the conflict were not ethnic, but that the old communist regime persistently tried (and to some extent succeeded) in using the conflict to create ethnic antagonism.

Central Asia is a region of incredible ethnic variety and intermingling. It is thus a region in which outsiders expect to see ethnic conflict and, when conflicts broke out in the post-soviet period, they were promptly labeled as ethnic. As we have seen, these disputes arose largely as a result of the destruction of a working multiethnic system and the consequent artificial divisions between centers and hinterlands, leading to rival claims to resources (Barfield 1994: 50–51). Meanwhile, it is significant that the new Central Asian states granted citizenship to their entire populations, regardless of their ethnicity or fluency in the language of the titular nationality. This is in accordance

---

9. See Schoeberlein-Engel in press.

with the Central Asian tradition described in this section of accepting that different peoples can live together in mutually interdependent plural societies. The soviet attempt to break up these interethnic arrangements and rearrange them along ethnic lines has not so much pitted nationalities against each other as it has destroyed the traditionally interdependent use of resources and thus created acute resource competition throughout the region.

China[10]

National Minorities

China has been a multinational state for thousands of years. In the course of its long history it was sometimes conquered by nomadic invaders from Central Asia. It was this constant threat that prompted Chinese rulers to build the Great Wall to protect the rich, settled agricultural areas of China proper against the marauders from the west. The Mongols and others who conquered China settled in China, set up their own dynasties, and eventually adopted Chinese ways. On the whole, however, it was the Han Chinese themselves who used the power and organization of the Chinese kingdom to conquer neighboring peoples and bring them under Chinese rule. In this way, China came to have a large number of non-Han peoples within its territory. Traditionally Chinese rule over these peoples was indirect. The ruler of a subject people was expected to acknowledge the Chinese emperor as his overlord and pay tribute to him. The Chinese would then appoint a kind of viceroy to the subject people, who sat with their ruler, but normally interfered very little, allowing the local people to run their own affairs as they had been accustomed to do.

These neighboring peoples who were absorbed into the Chinese system were traditionally considered barbarians in need of civilizing, and some of them did indeed adopt Chinese customs over time. Others, like the Tibetans, have fiercely held to their own ways. Chinese historians of the communist period have nevertheless tended to portray these peripheral populations as peoples who came into the Chinese orbit and, except for a few reactionaries in their midst, accepted Chinese ways once it was possible for them to do so. As a result, they are all considered Chinese peoples, though not Han.

China, according to this reasoning, includes all those peoples who belong or *have belonged* to the Chinese family of nations. Taiwanese are

---

10. The material in this section is drawn principally from Heberer 1989 and Mackerras 1994.

clearly part of China, as the Taiwanese themselves (except for the indigenous inhabitants of the island) agree, even though they are not at the moment part of the Chinese polity. The people of Korea and Outer Mongolia are also considered to be "temporarily" outside of the Chinese fold, to which they properly and historically belong. Likewise Tibet is considered unequivocally part of China, which is why the government of the People's Republic of China is willing to consider any Tibetan grievance except a demand for independence.

These views reflect the idea of a Han civilization that has done other peoples a favor by drawing them into its orbit and causing them to be sinified, a process that is thought to be both beneficial and irreversible. So, when Sun Yat Sen established the Chinese republic after the fall of the last weak Ching dynasty in 1911, he included Mongolians, Manchu, Tibetans, and Moslems among the Chinese, and urged that they should be gradually and fully assimilated in the interests of the nation. His successor, Chiang Kai-shek, denied that these peoples even constituted different nationalities, insisting that they were "branch clans" of the Han (Heberer 1989: 18). They still needed to be properly assimilated, but in Chiang Kai-shek's view needed little by way of special treatment.

It should be clear by now that the Chinese idea of "nationality" is rather different from the normal connotations of that term in English. The word in Chinese is *minzu*, which can refer to concepts that would be distinguished in English as ethnic group or *people*, or *nationality* or *nation*. They do, however, distinguish all nationalities in China, other than the Han, as *shaoshu minzu*, which is normally translated as *national minority*. Such national minorities are relatively small compared to the Han and possess certain characteristics that distinguish them as separate peoples.

Until quite recently it was not at all clear how many of these minorities existed within China, so in the 1950s the new communist government began to investigate. Four hundred ethnic groups responded to the initial call to register as a national minority but, after the government's ethnologists had worked with them for some years, it was decided that there was reduplication among the claimants. The scholars discovered that many who claimed to be of separate nationalities actually belonged to a single group that had been dispersed over the years. Others belonged to the same people, different subgroups of which used different names. There were even groups applying for recognition as minorities who were Han but had become isolated and lost any sense of their origins.[11]

---

11. For a discussion of the extraordinary complexities of trying to identify and classify national minorities, see Heberer 1989: 34–35 and 38–39.

As a result of this scholarly investigation and the administrative actions that stemmed from it, fifty-five national minorities were recognized in China that, together with the Han, make a total of fifty-six nationalities. The Han are an overwhelming majority. According to the census of 1990, there were over a billion Han or 92 percent of the population. The non-Han minorities between them had a substantial population of more than 91 million people, but it represented only 8 percent of the total. Meanwhile more than three-quarters of a million people remain unclassified according to the censuses![12]

On the other hand, the national minorities inhabit more than half of China's total territory, especially in its outlying border regions, which are not only strategically significant but contain rich deposits of raw materials.

In the early years of the communist regime, there was much discussion of how to define a nationality, how to identify one, and what treatment was appropriate for national minorities. The new regime was much more inclined to be tolerant of differences and to permit some autonomy to national minorities than were their republican predecessors. Their Han chauvinism set them at odds with those minorities whom they could control and led the Muslim areas of China's far west in Xinjiang to rebellion and outright, though temporary, secession in 1944. Official communist policy was, by contrast, to guarantee the rights of dispersed minorities and to grant some local autonomy to regional ones. The policy was never effectively implemented, though, and the traditional Han tendency to steer minority peoples towards assimilation continued. These pressures were dramatically increased at the time of the cultural revolution, launched by Mao Zedong in 1966. The broad outlines of this drastic revolution within a revolution are well known. Mao launched the movement to combat what he considered to be the growing conservatism (or what he called the "bourgeois penetration") of his communist revolution, and authorized young troops of Red Guards to root out and deal with backsliders and those who disagreed with his own vision of where the revolution should be headed. The effects on the Chinese economy and society were catastrophic, and the effects on the national minorities even more so.

Gone were the hesitations about the correct policy to adopt toward national minorities. The Red Guards, now speaking for the future, insisted that China was not a multinational country and that there was therefore no need to have any special policy for minorities. These were not to enjoy any local autonomy (which was condemned

---

12. For recent population figures on China's nationalities, see Mackerras 1994: 238–240.

as dividing the nation) and the resources of their regions were to be developed by the central planners in Beijing for the good of the country as a whole. Meanwhile, the customs of minority peoples were censured or forbidden. Most of them were forbidden to speak their languages or use their own scripts, if they had them. Mongolian, Tibetan, Uigur, Kazakh, and Korean scripts were permitted to continue but their use was severely restricted. Most schools that taught minorities in their own languages were abolished. The healing practices (and practitioners) among minority peoples were condemned, as were their traditions, their art, their literature, and their music.

After Mao's death and the ending of the cultural revolution, the regime reverted to its previous policies toward national minorities, but the minorities were now tired of the unkept promises of previous decades and bitter over the abuses they had suffered during the cultural revolutionary frenzy. They tended to hold the Han majority responsible for those abuses, even though they had been inflicted by one faction of Han on Han and non-Han alike. In 1980, they demanded that their grievances be redressed, and in 1984, legislation was passed giving further guarantees of autonomy and self-administration to national minorities.

The problem remains, as always, with the implementation. As long as these legislative guarantees can be overridden by the communist party "in the national interest," then they continue to offer very little protection for minority rights. There appear to be two continuing tendencies that militate against the minorities. Han chauvinism is alive and well. The customs of national minorities are regularly under Han scrutiny and it is Han administrators who decide which customs are "healthy" and should be allowed to continue and which are "unhealthy" and should be forbidden. This policy, combined with caution and insensitivity in the government bureaucracy, is a constant threat to minority cultures. The second threat comes from Han notions of development, which often involve sponsoring intensive Han migration into minority regions and development of extractive and other industries in those areas, with little consultation with or concern for the minority populations already living there.

Secession: The Case of Tibet

The Tibetans are the only national minority who have systematically demanded the right to secede from China and establish their own independent state. They justify this in terms of Chinese repression in the present and a history of Tibetan independence in the past. This history can be briefly summarized as follows.

Tibetans first made military incursions into China in the sixth century AD. They were later combined with China by the Mongols who conquered and ruled both countries in the thirteenth century. From the late fourteenth century onward, Tibet recognized Chinese suzerainty and paid tribute to the Chinese emperors, but essentially ran its own affairs. In the late nineteenth century, Britain and Russia were competing for power and influence in Central Asia when the Chinese empire was at its weakest. It was with British support that Tibet drove out the Chinese and declared itself independent in 1911, at the time when Sun Yat Sen's revolution in China brought down the last imperial dynasty. During the second world war, with China fighting for its existence against the Japanese, Tibet asked for worldwide recognition as an independent country, but this was not forthcoming. It was retaken by the victorious Chinese communist army in 1950.

The Tibetans were once again promised local autonomy, this time under Chinese communist suzerainty; but they rose up in revolt when the communists imposed social and land reforms in Tibet at the time of the Great Leap Forward in 1958. In 1959, the Dalai Lama and thousand of Tibetans went into exile in India. Tibet was even more seriously ravaged by the cultural revolution than other parts of China, for the Red Guards did their best to abolish the culture and institutions of a people whom they considered backward and disloyal. Now, after China his disavowed the cultural revolution, Tibet is still affected by what many Tibetans consider to be a Chinese "occupation" and by the flood of Han migrants who are being resettled in their country or province, whichever way one looks at it.

It is difficult to see how the Tibetan view of their situation can be reconciled at present with the Chinese one. According to the Chinese theory of nationality outlined earlier, Tibet is clearly part of China and has been for most of its history. The Tibetans, for their part, contend that Tibet wishes to regain an independence that it enjoyed in the past and that it has a right to demand because Tibetan rights— their human rights and their right to their own culture—are being infringed by the Chinese in the present.

Marginal Nationalities

The situation of Chinese national minorities is thus very different from that of nationalities in the former Soviet Union (FSU). Although the communist authorities have often claimed to grant autonomy to the national minorities in the People's Republic of China (PRC), there was never any formal division of the nation as a whole into ethnic regions as there was in the FSU. At the same time, Han chauvinism, Chinese tradition, and the overwhelming majority in numbers that the Han enjoy as compared with the national minorities have all contributed to maintain a strong assimilationist tradition in China.

The policies of the PRC toward its minorities strongly resemble the policies adopted by some of the countries described in Chapter 1 toward their indigenous peoples. Similar arguments have been used in both cases. According to these arguments, the minorities are barbarians to be civilized. Likewise, the Chinese during the cultural revolution and the governments of melting-pot societies in the western hemisphere argue that minorities should not be formally recognized or encouraged to maintain their cultures because that would divide and harm the nation. Similarly, both parties insist that if minorities occupy territory that contains natural resources, then the government has the right to exploit those resources for the good of the nation as a whole, even if that brings hardship to the minorities.

There is one final overarching similarity. Indigenous people are, by definition, marginal to the state, and the national minorities of China tend to be too. They are for the most part located in peripheral areas that are nevertheless strategically and economically important. Their location raises concerns about the security of the nation's frontiers, especially if there is any likelihood that they might secede. Tibet raises this question directly, but it is also of some concern in the western regions of China, an area inhabited by Muslim speakers of Turkic languages, who might also secede (as they did in 1944) or join up with others like them across the border with the FSU.

So far, the response of the PRC to these concerns has been to promise regional autonomy to national minorities but to continue its assimilationist policies at the same time, particularly by encouraging massive Han immigration into nominally minority regions.

ETHNICITY WITHIN THE SYSTEM

In this section I discuss two countries that have succeeded in allowing ethnicity to be expressed within their social and political systems without destabilizing the state in order to see what lessons can be drawn from their experiences.

Indonesia[13]

Indonesia is an extraordinary country whose ethnic diversity is matched only by India's. Its population of about 185 million people is made up of approximately 300 ethnic groups inhabiting nearly half of the islands in an archipelago of some 14,000 islands that cover an

---

13. The material in this section is largely drawn from Aragon 1994 and Kipp 1993.

area as broad as the United States (see map on p. xiv). The peoples inhabiting these islands all had only one thing in common when Indonesia proclaimed its independence in 1945 after the second world war—the experience of Dutch rule. Indonesia as a state defined itself geographically as occupying the territory of what had been the Dutch East Indies. It faced an acute problem of nation building as it attempted to inculcate a sense of common nationality in scattered peoples with little sense of a common history, who were now all citizens of a newly independent, post-colonial state.

It had one great advantage over other multiethnic, post-colonial states—its first president, Sukarno, established one single, noncontroversial language as the national language. This was called *bahasa Indonesia* or the Indonesian language and was based on a dialect of Malay that had been used throughout the islands as a lingua franca—a language for trade—in colonial times. The advantage of bahasa Indonesia was that it was not the language of any large or influential group within the country. In particular, it was not Javanese. Since the island of Java has a population now of over 100 million people, 70 percent of whom are Javanese, the imposition of Javanese as the national language would have been resented as a sign of Javanese hegemony. Although Indonesia started out with a national language, the nation was from the beginning riven with regional and political conflicts. There were regional revolts in the early years of the new republic, although whether they were aiming for secession or for greater power within the state is still a matter of debate. These revolts were effectively put down by the military, whose power and self-confidence was much improved as a result; but the watershed in Indonesia's independent history came in 1965. By this time, Sukarno, the charismatic leader of the new nation, was treading a fine line as he tried to keep a balance of power between the army and the PKI (Communist Party of Indonesia), which was spearheading the left-wing populist opposition within the country. In 1965 six generals were kidnapped and murdered in an attempted coup. The PKI insisted that it was the result of an internal conflict within the military. The military blamed the PKI, with whom they felt that President Sukarno had become altogether too friendly. General Suharto and his army units unleashed a purge of the PKI and of Chinese Indonesians who were suspected of being fellow-travelers (Communist in all but name). A frenzy of killing followed, which traumatized the country. Nobody can be quite sure how many were massacred, but estimates range from under half a million to a million people. The PKI was effectively eliminated as political force, which weakened Sukarno's position. In 1966 he was forced to delegate power to Suharto and the army. In 1968 Suharto became president and Sukarno was placed under house arrest until his death in 1970.

Sukarno's economic policies had led to hyperinflation and huge foreign debt in Indonesia. The hardships this imposed on ordinary Indonesians had much to do with the strength of the PKI. Accordingly, the new regime stressed economic development and made this the special responsibility of the Javanese-dominated army. It also emphasized moral development, which was to be implemented by carrying out policies that Sukarno had invented for the new nation. These were inspired by *pancasila* or the Five Principles of the official philosophy that Sukarno had proposed for Indonesia. The *pancasila* and a celebration of ethnic diversity were to be taught through intensive programs of education in the schools and the mass media.

The official slogan of the country is "Unity in Diversity," in the name of which the government does a great deal to encourage the myriad ethnic groups of Indonesia to put their distinctive ethnicities on display. The outward aspects of cultural differences—songs, dances, arts and crafts, house styles, and even burial customs (as among the Toradja, whose cliff burials are spectacular both as ceremonies and as sites to visit)—have, with official support, become a showcase for Indonesian diversity. President Suharto and his wife personally sponsored the building in the capital city of Jakarta of a "Beautiful Indonesia in Miniature" theme park inspired by Disneyland. The park has a display featuring a traditional house from a representative ethnic group from every province in the country, furnished with typical artifacts. The houses are arranged around a central Javanese-style auditorium containing miniature replicas of the nation's treasures. As Aragon points out (1994: 74), the symbolic message of the park indicates not only the ethnic richness and cultural diversity of Indonesia, but also the control exercised from the center over the very identities of ethnic minorities.

The tension between encouragement and control of ethnicity has been noted by most writers on Indonesia. The government encourages ethnic diversity, but this also gives it the opportunity to support local leaders whose conservative stake in state-sponsored ethnicity makes them supporters of the system. Local aristocrats and others thus receive support from the central government in a policy that resembles the divide and rule tactics of the Dutch and has similar effects.

The other ideological pillar of the regime is Sukarno's Five Principles or *pancasila*, to which all Indonesians are expected to subscribe. They are: belief in a supreme God, humanitarianism, national unity, democracy, and social justice. The first principle is in some ways the most significant. It serves to exclude from the national fold atheists (and therefore communists). It also serves to restrain Muslim fundamentalists by enshrining religion as a central necessity for all Indonesians, but refusing to admit or permit the superiority of any one religion over others. In so doing it legitimates the Hindu, Buddhist, and Christian (of various denominations) minorities within the country and forestalls the hopes of those in the Muslim majority who might wish to turn Indonesia into an Islamic nation.

It also provides a rationale for "civilizing" marginal, indigenous peoples by requiring them to abandon their "superstitions" and convert to one of the faiths that are considered in Indonesia to be essentially monotheistic. In fact, the "indigenous" or tribal peoples of Indonesia are distinguished from other ethnic groups largely because they do not subscribe to any of the major religions. They do, of course, live in relatively remote regions and are socially and economically marginal to Indonesian society, but the religious difference is in Indonesia their most salient distinguishing characteristic. Because the most active missionaries in Indonesia have always been Christian, there has been a certain tendency to allow the Christians to carry out the religious part of the "civilizing" process among such peoples.

Pancasila is the cornerstone of Indonesian education. Required courses in it are taught in schools and in the universities. Refresher courses in it are required of civil servants. It has, in fact, become a full-fledged ideology, which disturbs devout Muslims who see it being promoted as virtually an official religion. In fact, when the government introduced a law in 1986 requiring that *pancasila* be the sole foundation of all "mass organizations," this raised questions among Christians as well as Muslims (Kipp 1993: 107–8), for whom "belief in a supreme God" is a necessary but not sufficient part of their own belief systems.

Pancasila underlies a certain view of morality and of Indonesian society, so that courses in *pancasila* are simultaneously courses in ethics and civics. *Pancasila* also serves as a bulwark against what the regime perceives as the two most serious threats to it, namely those (defined as communists) who oppose the government because it presides over enormous inequities of wealth, and those (devout Muslims) who oppose the government because it allows too much materialism. The communists are defined as beyond the pale because they do not believe in God, and *pancasila* is used against Muslim fundamentalists by showing that the government supports a strong morality in the population, but not to the extent of permitting intolerance.

Tolerance is, in effect, a central tenet of the official ideology and its incorporation, together with *pancasila,* in the national ideology was for a time effective in helping Indonesia avoid the kinds of ethnic and sectarian conflicts that might otherwise have plagued such a diverse society. The government moved decades ago to prohibit speech or actions that denigrated other peoples or religions, a measure that is part of its careful management of interethnic relations throughout the country. Meanwhile, the official presentation of Indonesian diversity as harmonious and unifying does serve to disguise other aspects of interethnic relations that are potentially more explosive, particularly the numerical and political domination by the Javanese and the commercial domination by the Chinese.

The perception of Javanese hegemony was particularly dangerous when the government was sponsoring large transmigration programs intended to transfer people from the densely overpopulated inner islands, especially from Java, to the thinly populated outer islands, such as Sumatra or Kalimantan. Transmigrants were also being sent *en masse* to Irian Jaya in order to de-Papuanize Indonesia's part of New Guinea.[14]

The affluence of the Chinese business community is a difficult issue for the government because it needs the Chinese and their connections. Indeed, many high-ranking officials depend on income from their Chinese business partners, but the government also realizes that the position of the Chinese causes resentment among ordinary Indonesians. They have long disliked them as affluent aliens and, more recently, have demonized them as communist fellow-travelers suspected of bankrolling the PKI. It is noticeable that the Chinese do not figure at all in the official portrayals of ethnic diversity, although many of them have lived in Indonesia for generations and some no longer even speak Chinese (Kipp 1993: 116–17).

The Indonesian government has been engaged for a long time in a delicate balancing act. It has encouraged Indonesians to take pride in the diversity of their country and to believe that "Unity in Diversity" is no empty slogan. Yet its exhibitions of ethnic diversity, like all exhibitions, are concealing as well as revealing. By presenting a vision of diverse peoples creating national unity, they disguise Javanese dominance in the political bureaucracy; and by treating the Chinese as if they did not exist, they hide Chinese dominance in business. At the same time, the nation is constantly urged to be vigilant against communism, which virtually ceased to exist in Indonesia when the present regime came to power by crushing it in 1965. As Kipp points out (1993: 121–2) the calls for anticommunist vigilance seem to indicate a class-based anxiety about inequalities in Indonesian society, which are obliquely alluded to as not-yet-solved "problems of social justice."

Even the much vaunted ethnic harmony, which has been such an integral part of the nation's self-image since the slaughter of the suspected communists, appears to have been a fragile peace maintained by the authoritarian control exercised by President Suharto and the

---

14. See Chapter 1.

military. By 1997, there was widespread unrest in Indonesia as people protested against the economic mismanagement and corruption of the Suharto regime. By 1998, people were not only rioting against the regime, but they were also attacking the Chinese communities in the country's major cities. Meanwhile, fighting broke out between Christians and Muslims in various parts of the country. Suharto finally resigned from the presidency, which was taken over by his vice president Habibie. This did not pacify the protestors, however, for they felt that Habibie was too closely tied to Suharto to be able to mount a credible investigation into the massive corruption and diversion of the country's wealth to Suharto's family and friends, of which the previous regime stood accused. A measure of political peace was restored only when Habibie resigned and Abdurrahman Wahid took over as president in 1999. However, at the time of writing, Wahid's presidency is already in trouble. Legislators are dissatisfied with his erratic style of leadership and with his inability to deal with the economic problems and the various separatist rebellions and local ethnic conflicts that are simmering throughout the country. He has therefore been censured by parliament.

To sum up, President Suharto's regime, which defined modern Indonesia, was launched in a massacre and operated by means of corruption and military control. Yet, for decades it was successful at nation building and avoiding ethnic conflict while encouraging a climate of ethnic tolerance. For a while, it was also successful in diverting its citizens' attention from other problems, which threatened the stability it so painstakingly cultivated. This was not, however, so much a result of teaching tolerance as it was of systematic repression that prevented conflicts from being expressed in interethnic terms.

Spain[15]

Spain furnishes an interesting contrast to Indonesia because it has managed to accommodate multiethnicity without resorting to authoritarianism. Spain has a long regionalist tradition dating back to the middle ages. The country is conventionally thought to have been united by the marriage of the so-called Catholic Kings—Ferdinand of Aragon and Isabella of Castile—in 1469. It was an article of faith with General Franco, who ruled Spain dictatorially from 1936–1975, and still is an article of faith with people on the right wing of Spanish politics today that the golden age of Spanish grandeur was a direct

---

15. The materials in this section are drawn primarily from Aretxaga 1994 and Gilmour 1985.

result of this unification. In this view, the Catholic Kings, leading a united Spain, ushered in the era when the last of the Moors were defeated and expelled, when Spanish armies were invincible in Europe, and Spain not only helped to fight off the Turks but also conquered and "Christianized" a vast empire in the Americas. Spain did indeed do all these things, but it is a misreading of the historical record to claim that they resulted from the unification of the country, for that was not fully accomplished until the early eighteenth century (Gilmour 1985: 106–9). In fact, both before and after its formal unification, Spain was home to strong regionalist traditions.

The medieval arrangements that permitted different regions of the peninsula to keep their own customs, control their own affairs, and even decide how much they should pay the central government in taxes were maintained over the centuries. They came to be jealously protected, especially in the regions of the Basque provinces and Catalonia, whose inhabitants spoke their own languages and insisted on their ethnic separateness from the areas where Spanish was spoken. Some Basque nationalists have, in fact, maintained that their part of Spain was never conquered by Romans, Moors, or Castilians. According to this view, the Basques came into the Spanish monarchy of their own free will, and their privileges could not therefore be abolished by outsiders because they are among the institutions of a free and sovereign people.

When General Franco took power in 1936, he set about abolishing these regionalist and separatist tendencies once and for all, or so he thought. He centralized the government and ruled Spain's regions through governors responsible to Madrid. His repression was especially severe in the Basque country and Catalonia. He forbade the teaching of Basque or Catalan in schools and prohibited all publications in either language. In Catalonia, which is industrially the most developed area of Spain, Franco's administration actually hindered production by controlling factory output and withholding export licenses to enable the other regions of Spain to catch up (Gilmour 1985: 120–22). The repression, tortures, and other penalties inflicted on Basque and Catalan nationalists merely served to strengthen the determination of these populations to maintain their own languages and cultures. It was this determination, accompanied by strong sentiments for autonomy, if not outright secession, that confronted the democratic government of Spain in the transitional phase immediately after Franco's death.

Franco had tried hard to recreate the centralized, united Spain of his historical imagination and to arrange to be succeeded by people who would continue to implement this vision of the country. He decided, eventually, that the restoration of the monarchy would be the most appropriate means of assuring the conservative continuity in

Spain that he hoped would follow after him. Because he did not trust the exiled pretender to the Spanish throne, he groomed the latter's son, Juan Carlos, to take over in his stead. When Franco died and Juan Carlos came to the throne in 1975, he found that his parliamentary government faced a quandary.

Spain had changed and modernized considerably since 1936, in spite of Franco's regime, and Catalonia and the Basque country, the two most industrialized regions of the nation, were chafing at the bit. After Franco's death, there were massive demonstrations in both regions demanding the restoration of their lost rights. At the same time, there were plenty of Franco supporters in parliament, and particularly in the army, for whom any thought of decentralization was anathema. The government felt it had to move slowly in granting the concessions demanded by the Basques and the Catalans, which merely fuelled the impatience of the latter and made them suspect that Madrid was not really serious about regional autonomy. It was a situation in which the government walked a fine line between ethnic violence if it failed to deal with the question of autonomy, and a military coup if it tried to.

Ethnic violence had in fact already broken out even before the death of Franco. The Basque nationalist movement had divided into factions, one of which advocated guerilla warfare to bring down the dictatorship and secure the independence of the Basque country. In 1968 it started to assassinate policemen and others associated with the regime. Franco responded by intensifying the repression of the Basques, which produced a cycle of violence and repression while the Basque extremists became heroes to their own people (Gilmour 1985: 129). The attacks by Basque extremists continued after the death of Franco, for they did not believe that the civilian government was going to grant independence to Euskadi (the Basque name for their own country). Meanwhile, moderate Basques were slow to condemn them because the police in newly democratic Spain continued to use the totalitarian methods that they had practiced for so long under the old regime. So, if moderate Basques were outraged when their countrypeople, for example, blew up a cafe in Madrid, this outrage was quickly dissipated by their disgust on learning that the police had yet again been torturing and murdering Basque suspects.

This "dirty war," with the army waiting in the wings, was therefore the climate in which the government was trying to negotiate some sort of autonomy for the dissatisfied regions. In the meantime, conservatives and the military were openly and publicly contemptuous of the new democratic regime, however gently it tried to treat them. Fortunately, when the threatened coup was actually carried out it was under the leadership of a general who felt that the transition to democracy had brought only "terrorism, insecurity, inflation, economic crisis, pornography and, above all, a crisis of authority."[16] It failed. It was carried out in the name of the king, but he surprised the military by opposing it and rallying enough officers to his view so that the coup could not succeed.

Post-Franco Spain was now called on to devise modern solutions for a country in which four languages and several dialects are spoken. The languages are Basque, Galician, Catalan, and Spanish. The last three are related Latin languages, but Basque is not even of the same language family.[17] The country is divided into five major regions: Basque Provinces-Navarre (or Euskadi), Galicia, and Catalonia, each with its own language; and Castile and Andalucia, which are Spanish speaking.

At long last, regional autonomy was in fact granted to both Euskadi and Catalonia; the Basque extremists found themselves increasingly isolated and the incidence of violence diminished. The government then decided to decentralize its administration and made complicated arrangements for regional elections. These resulted eventually in regional autonomy for all the regions of Spain, including those which had not requested it and whose inhabitants spoke Spanish and saw themselves as part of mainstream Spanish culture.

The return of considerable autonomy to the regions has the double advantage of being a solution hallowed by a long Spanish tradition and of satisfying the demands of the majority of Basques and Catalans, but it is a solution that is still opposed by the majority of Spanish conservatives.

Nor are the conservatives the only ones to challenge it. The autonomy negotiations and the decentralized system of governance were put into effect by a government of Spain's socialist party. That party began slipping in the polls in the mid-1990s due to the high levels of inflation and unemployment affecting the country. The socialists were also tainted by a number of scandals, not the least of which was the revelation that, under their administration, the police had continued the "dirty war" against presumed Basque terrorists.

On the other side, though moderate Basques supported the local autonomy arrangements, the militant wing of the Basque separatist movement kept up its bombings and murderous attacks on civilians

---

16. Quoted in Gilmour 1985: 241.
17. In fact nobody has succeeded in establishing definite connections between Basque and any other language, or even prehistoric connections between the Basques and any other people.

(including Basque civilians) in pursuit of their goal of total independence for the Basque country. Even Catalan separatists detonated bombs for the same purpose. The government of Spain has therefore found itself embroiled in protracted, anti-guerilla warfare, even after putting into effect the solutions that were supposed to satisfy all but the most diehard separatists.

CONCLUSION

Certain interesting themes emerge from the cases discussed in this chapter. They showed at least two models of interethnic accommodation that have long histories. The idea of granting local autonomy to peoples living in and owing allegiance to the Spanish state goes back to the middle ages. Even though such autonomy has not always been granted, and at times has been passionately rejected, the conflicting claims of regionalism (together with limited autonomy for ethnic groups) and centralism have been debated in Spain for centuries, and the debate still continues.

A different kind of interethnic system seems to have arisen spontaneously in Central Asia. There, a variety of peoples lived and interacted with each other under the loose control of the Khans who ruled from the major cities. This was a form of control that seems old-fashioned nowadays, when modern states have more sophisticated means of communication, organization, and coercion at their disposal. Indeed, it was old-fashioned at the time, compared, for example, to the control exercised a little bit farther west by the expanding Tsarist empire.

That empire, by contrast, administered its subject peoples in ordinary colonialist fashion, trying to persuade or coerce them to adopt Russian ways and to orient their production toward commodities that benefited the Russian empire. The Chinese empire likewise fully intended to sinify its subject peoples or, as they would have said, those peoples who had now been brought into the fold of Chinese civilization.

When the communists took over, both in Russia and in China, their nationalities policies ostensibly made a break with the past. Both regimes admitted that they governed multiethnic states in which peoples of various ethnicities (or nationalities) were to be allowed to maintain their distinctiveness, speak their own languages, continue to practice their own customs, and have considerable control of their own local affairs. But the practice was very different from the theory.

In China, increasing control was exercised from the center over national minorities until the cultural revolution, when their very right to exist was denied. Since the death of Mao, some rights have been returned to national minorities, but strong central control still remains.

Similarly, in the former Soviet Union, a facade of ethnic independence concealed the arbitrary control exercised from Moscow over the supposedly autonomous peoples. Nevertheless, because the whole administration of the soviet state was theoretically based on the principle of giving each people within the union its own territory, the idea of ethnic territories became firmly established. It is this idea, combined with Stalin's manipulations of ethnic groups and their territories, that has created the modern situation where ethnic groups are trying to unscramble themselves and to resolve competing claims to territories and resources. Furthermore, it is in this situation that the people I have called "ethnic entrepreneurs" (borrowing a phrase from Valery Tishkov) have come into their own. Most of them are old communists who found their positions threatened and careers blocked by the collapse of both the ideology they had championed and of the state that had forced people to accept it. They, therefore, reinvented themselves as nationalist leaders, which enabled them to hang onto power in the post-soviet chaos.

The two salient factors in the production of ethnic conflict would seem from these cases to be the ethnic definition of the state (or of a territory within the state) and the activity of ethnic entrepreneurs, who are willing to play on and use ethnic distinctions to create conflict and eventually "ethnic cleansing."

Why, we might ask at this stage, did the allocation of ethnic territories in the former Soviet Union contribute to ethnic conflict, when in Spain it seems to have been a solution that has had some success in putting an end to it? Apart from the obvious differences between the two cases and the much greater ethnic complexity of the former Soviet Union, there is a more interesting conclusion to be drawn from this comparison. Local autonomy for ethnic groups promotes interethnic harmony only when it is part of an interethnic system that functions reasonably well. Under these circumstances, members of the non-titular nationalities in a given territory know what their rights are and they have somewhere else to go within the system if they are not satisfied. This is true in Spain but much less so in the former Soviet Union.

In other words, a system that avoids ethnic conflict might need a combination of the two models with which I opened this section. It needs to guarantee local autonomy to groups that have reason to insist on it, but, at the same time, it needs to guarantee that this autonomy is not exercised in an exclusive and isolationist fashion vis-à-vis other people in the wider society. It needs to try to institutionalize some kind of routine and harmonious interethnic connectedness, which is what the Central Asians had succeeded in doing before they were incorporated into the soviet state.

The Indonesian case is interesting because it highlights the advantages of providing systematic, state-sponsored education in ethnic tolerance, together with a nationally enforced ban on "hate speech" and incitement to ethnic violence. Yet the banning of "hate speech," which I shall discuss in Chapter 5, is a difficult and contentious issue in most democratic countries and often has unfortunate consequences that are far from those intended. At the same time, we noted that the Indonesian solution was underwritten by an authoritarian military regime that suppressed serious opposition and kept President Suharto in power for twenty-seven years. Most societies would find this too high a price to pay for ethnic peace, yet, in all fairness, most societies do not contain the kaleidoscope of different ethnic groups that Indonesia does.

The underlying theme of all these cases seems to be control. Is it only possible to avoid ethnic conflict if firm control is exercised by the state over the peoples who might otherwise do battle with each other? That would be a depressing conclusion and not even a guaranteed solution at that, for the soviet state exercised the most ferocious control of all and this had the effect of virtually incubating ethnic conflicts within it. I do not believe that the prospects for interethnic harmony in the future are quite that desperate, but before I discuss the reasons for my guarded optimism, we need to analyze two recent horror stories—two worst-case scenarios—where ethnic divergences have led to slaughter on a large scale.

3

Genocide and Ethnic Cleansing

There is a widespread fear of ethnicity throughout the world. It is thought to lead to divisiveness and discord, to fragment society, and to undermine the state. It is generally associated, as we have seen, with conflict; not just with ordinary conflict, but with especial horrors that can lead to ethnic cleansing and the obscenity of genocide. These are the ultimate disasters that may be visited on a society in which ethnic conflict is allowed (or, worse still, encouraged) to escalate beyond the point of no return. These are the specters that haunt our post–cold war imagination of a world in which disorder runs rampant. In this chapter I shall consider two recent examples of ethnic conflict and mass slaughter in order to see whether they confirm these gloomy forebodings.

RWANDA[1]

Even in this genocidal age, the mass killings in Burundi and more recently in Rwanda have seemed particularly shocking. It was not just the extent of the carnage. Somewhere between half a million and a million people were killed in Rawanda in April 1994, more than twice as many as in the first two years of the war in Bosnia. Nor was it the manner of the killing, with hundreds upon thousands of people being speared, clubbed, or literally hacked to pieces. Even more horrifying was the fact that this was a planned and organized slaughter, well known in advance, about which the international community took no preventive action. Indeed, that same community responded

---

1. The material in this section is drawn principally from de Waal 1994, Fein 1994, and Lemarchand 1994.

only hesitantly after the killing had been done, and in some cases continued to support the killers.

One reason why no one was willing to intervene to prevent this genocide was that it was presented to the world at large as another instance of tribal warfare. The Tutsi and the Hutu have always been killing each other, so it was believed, and there was not very much the rest of the world could (or perhaps even should) do about it. This was a total misunderstanding, but a misunderstanding that allowed the genocide to proceed in full view of a world that was reluctant to stop it. The circumstances leading up to the massacres are at once more complex and more revealing.

The Central African territory known at that time as Ruanda-Urundi was ruled by Belgium from 1916 to 1962. In 1962 the northern part of the territory became the independent state of Rwanda and the southern part the independent state of Burundi (see map on p. xiii). The population of both countries was about one-fifth Tutsi and four-fifths Hutu, with between 1 and 2 percent being Twa. In pre-colonial times, this area was governed by Tutsi kings in a neofeudal system where Tutsi lords ruled over Hutu peasants, with the Twa considered aboriginals and therefore at the bottom of the heap. Colonial missionary historians interpreted this system as having originated with the arrival of tall, Nilo-Hamitic, light-skinned, cattle-owning Tutsi conquerors who established their sway over the stocky, Bantu, dark-skinned Hutu peasantry. In fact, the physical differences between the groups were much exaggerated by this colonial account of their origins that distinguished them as different racial types and went so far as to attribute the superiority of the Tutsi to their early exposure to Coptic Christianity in Ethiopia, their supposed place of origin.

This colonial and racial "explanation" of society in Ruanda-Urundi presented a distorted view of a system in which Tutsi, Hutu, and Twa speak the same language and share the same religion and culture. Moreover, it is rarely possible to tell whether individuals are Twa, Hutu, or Tutsi from their physical characteristics. In effect, the Europeans exaggerated the differences between people who were all part of a single system, and attributed these differences to their supposedly separate racial backgrounds.

What the colonialists had, in fact, encountered in Ruanda-Urundi was a hierarchical system in which Tutsi and Hutu were differentiated by social and occupational status[2] and the Twa were marginal. In the pre-colonial period of the early nineteenth century, *Tutsi* was a term applied to lineages that controlled wealth (particularly in cattle)

---

2. See de Waal 1994: 1–2 and Lemarchand 1994: 30–31.

and power. Tutsi lineages were linked to powerful chiefs. Hutu lineages were those who did not possess wealth and were not closely tied to the powerful. Poor Tutsi could slide into being considered Hutu, and wealthy Hutu lineages would, over time, come to be considered Tutsi (Newbury 1988: 11).

The Tutsi were an aristocracy maintained by a Hutu peasantry. The land and cattle of a peasant could at any time be confiscated by a powerful chief, unless the peasant was protected by another chief. Hutu would therefore become clients of Tutsi chiefs and pay them for their protection, because the risk of remaining independent was to lose everything. Because there were numerous chiefs and they were arranged in no formal hierarchy—the Tutsi king or *Mwami* was simply the most powerful of the chiefs—a calculating Hutu had at least some options as to whose client he would become and to whom he could transfer his allegiance if it seemed advantageous.

This was the social system encountered first by the Germans and then by the Belgians as they penetrated this part of Africa at the end of the nineteenth century. When the Belgians eventually turned Ruanda-Urundi into a colony, they governed it by indirect rule. This meant that they supported the Tutsi aristocrats and administered the territory through them, thus giving the Tutsi more power than they had ever possessed in pre-colonial times. Tutsi rule under the Belgians, therefore, became much more onerous than it had been before. Yet even at this time, when the Belgians were giving the local social system an unwonted rigidity and then explaining the outcome as a result of racial differences, it was still difficult to tell individual Tutsi and Hutu apart. So the Belgians obliged everyone in the colony to carry an identity card that specified the group to which he or she belonged. Where there was doubt, a man owning ten or more head of cattle was classified as Tutsi, whereas one owning less was classified as Hutu!

The colonialist misinterpretation of this system was to have drastic consequences. In pre-colonial times there had been a certain reciprocity between the strata of society and even some possibility of individual upward mobility. This was destroyed by Belgian rule, which reinforced the authority of the Tutsi aristocracy and created a system of dominance and exploitation that succeeded in fragmenting the society. By the end of the colonial period, there was civil war between the Tutsi and the Hutu, who had now been officially separated into two distinct "ethnic groups." In Burundi, the Tutsi succeeded in crushing the Hutu rebellion and maintaining their hegemony, but in Rwanda, the Hutu emerged victorious and took control of the newly independent state. In 1972 the Tutsi rulers of Burundi moved to eliminate Hutu rebellion in a systematic slaughter of somewhere between 100,000 and 200,000 Hutu. Later, the reverse process in Rwanda pitted

Tutsi rebels against the Hutu-dominated regime. Many Tutsi went into exile in neighboring Uganda, where they created the Rwandese Popular Front or FPR.[3]

In Uganda, the FPR fought on the side of Yoweri Museveni and helped him to take power as president, for which they were rewarded, and some of their members became prominent in the Ugandan army. This Rwandan prominence came to be resented by native Ugandans, so President Museveni supported the FPR in their effort to fight their way back into Rwanda. The ongoing Rwandan civil war thus pitted the Hutu-dominated government of Rwanda, supported by France, against the Tutsi-dominated FPR, supported by Uganda.

It would be a mistake to believe that these forces represented a conflict between all Hutu and all Tutsi. On the contrary, as the war dragged on, there were many in both communities who wished for peace and collaboration between them. These desires, as well as international pressures, led to the signing of the Arusha accord in August 1993. This stipulated that a broadly based coalition government should be set up in Rwanda, including both Hutu and representatives of the FPR, until elections could be held twenty-two months later. Meanwhile, the Rwandan armed forces were to be reorganized so that 40 percent of their officers and 60 percent of their men were from the FPR.

Neighboring Burundi had meanwhile elected its first Hutu president, Melchior Ndadaye, after a transition to multi-party rule that brought to an end twenty-eight years of Tutsi hegemony. Ndadaye was enormously popular among the Hutu and had support among the Tutsi, so he promised at long last to bridge the divide between them. Sadly, this hope was killed by his assassination at the hands of the all-Tutsi army in October 1993.

Ndadaye's assassination had a direct influence on events in Rwanda. As violence swept Burundi, 200,000 panic-stricken Hutu fled across the border into Rwanda, where many of them were recruited into the rabidly anti-Tutsi militias that were already being formed. These militias were associated with two anti-Tutsi parties that were trying to undermine the Arusha accord and to destroy all those, both Hutu and Tutsi, who sought any compromise with the FPR. They were supported by the *akazu* death squads being organized by the inner circle of the president of Rwanda. The *akazu* (literally "little house") squads were organized, neighborhood by neighborhood, to identify Tutsi civilians who were marked for death. The only way that such people could be identified, supposing they did not produce

---

3. The initials of their name in French.

identity cards, was through the local knowledge that the *akazu* squads would provide. Meanwhile, President Habyalimana of Rwanda was systematically playing for time and postponing the implementation of the Arusha accord.

In April 1994, President Habyalimana went to Tanzania to attend UN-sponsored talks, which brought together the contending parties in Rwanda and the heads of other states in the region. He was now coming under intense pressure to implement the accord. When he returned to his own capital of Kigali along with the president of Burundi, their plane was shot out of the air by a surface-to-air missile as it was preparing to land. No one knows for sure who shot down the plane. The Rwandan government claimed that it was shot down by units of the Tutsi FPR, already stationed near Kigali as a first step in the implementation of the Arusha accord. The FPR, on the other hand, accused the Rwandan Presidential Guard itself of being the culprits, for they were doing everything in their power to undermine the Arusha accord and to set in motion the genocide that followed immediately.

As soon as news of the crash became known, the Presidential Guard set up road blocks around the capital and started to kill all Tutsi (and moderate Hutu who advocated cooperation with the Tutsi) including no less a figure than the Prime Minister of Rwanda herself, Agathe Umwilingiyimana, and other Hutu ministers. These events drew the FPR into the fray in a vain effort to stop the massacre. They were engaged by the Rwandan (Hutu) army in a long drawn out battle for Kigali while the slaughter of Hutu moderates and Tutsi continued behind the lines. In fact, as Alex de Waal pointed out (1994: 2), when the United Nations proposed sending troops to Rwanda to separate the contestants, this suited the Rwandan army very well. It would have given the Hutu extremists the opportunity to complete their genocidal work away from the battle lines. Eventually the FPR defeated the Rwandan (Hutu) army. This force withdrew, under international protection and with hundreds of thousands of refugees, into neighboring Zaïre. By that time, estimates of the dead exceeded half a million.

The retreat of the Hutu forces into Zaïre opened a new chapter in the Rwandan conflict. The Hutu forces controlled the refugee camps in eastern Zaïre with disastrous results. Many of the refugees wanted to take advantage of the Rwandan government's offer to allow those who had taken no part in the genocide to return, but they were prevented from doing so by their Hutu controllers who even carried out massacres of fellow refugees to enforce their control by terror (Leitenberg 1994: 41). These Rwandan soldiers hoped to retake control of their own country, a hope that was not as far-fetched as it might sound. They were waiting it out in Zaïre, secure in the knowledge that international resources were flowing to Zaïre for their maintenance, but few resources were flowing to the new government of Rwanda. The Rwandan government was short of money because the country was stripped of its resources by the retreating Hutu. When it appealed to the World Bank for funds, it was informed that, as successor to the previous regime, it would first have to pay the interest in arrears on Rwanda's debt. This led some in the FPR to remark that this must be the first time in history that people have been asked to pay interest on the funds borrowed to kill their relatives. Meanwhile France, which had all along supported the Hutu-dominated government of Rwanda, successfully blocked European aid to Rwanda for some time. Worst of all, Hutu in Zaïre have used the refugee camps and surrounding regions as staging areas for cross-border attacks on the Tutsi forces now controlling Rwanda.

Rwanda retaliated by supporting a rebel movement that sought to overthrow the government of Zaïre. Zaïre had been run by the kleptocratic regime of President Mobutu since 1965. The rebellion against Mobutu, supported by both Rwanda and Uganda, succeeded in deposing Mobutu in 1997 and replacing him with Laurent Kabila. Kabila changed the name of the nation back to what it had originally been called—the Democratic Republic of the Congo (DRC). The accession of Kabila did little, however, to bring peace to this troubled region. His government (and its Rwandan Tutsi allies) was quickly accused by human rights organizations of massacring Hutu refugees in the eastern part of the DRC. Soon after, the Rwandans decided that Kabila was no better than Mobutu. They felt he governed autocratically, seized the resources of the DRC for himself, and failed to rein in the Hutu who had crossed the border after the Rwandan genocide. So, the Rwandans and the Ugandans felt obliged to try to unseat Kabila and in fact succeeded in seizing the eastern half of Zaïre. Kabila was only saved by the intervention of Angola, Namibia, and Zimbabwe, all of whom sent troops to support him. This resulted in a stalemate, with Kabila and his allies controlling the western half of Zaïre while the Rwandans and their allies controlled the eastern half. At the time of writing, Laurent Kabila has been assassinated by his bodyguards and his son Joseph has assumed the presidency. Meanwhile, the stalemate continues.

It is clear that the repeated genocides in Rwanda and Burundi are not spontaneous eruptions of mutual hatred between contending ethnic groups. On the contrary, they have been influenced by foreign action and inaction. The Belgian colonial authorities, following European racial interpretations of society in this part of the world, gave a rigidity to the social system that it had never had before. They separated and reified categories like Tutsi, Hutu, and Twa, establishing them as distinct and mutually exclusive entities and exacerbating (if not creating) the antipathies between them. As Lemarchand put it

(1994: 31): "Now as in 1959 the root cause of ethnic violence must be found in the extent to which collective identities have been reactivated, mythologized and manipulated for political advantage. Hutu and Tutsi are not just ethnic labels,[4] but social categories which, arbitrary though they may be in some cases, carry an enormous emotional charge."

Hutu and Tutsi have, in effect, been separated from each other and then set against each other. Once this sinister dynamic had been set in motion, it was repeatedly used by extremists on both sides to bolster their political power. These extremists did not strive merely to annihilate the extremists on the other side, but also to eliminate moderates in the middle. They even targeted those among their own people who sought reconciliation or collaboration. Meanwhile, foreign countries have been willing to intervene when it suited their interests. Indeed, one of the remarkable aspects of the Rwandan genocide is that international inaction to prevent it has been matched by a widespread internationalization of the conflict.

At the time of the genocide, Uganda gave aid to the Tutsi-dominated FPR, as did France and Kenya to the then-Hutu-dominated government of Rwanda. The highest Hutu members of the Rwandan government fled to Kenya after the genocide and were protected there by President Arap Moi. Meanwhile, as we have seen, what began as a conflict between Hutu and Tutsi has spread throughout central Africa, involving, in addition to the countries already mentioned, the DRC, Angola, Namibia, and Zimbabwe.

The international community has, on the other hand, shown itself extraordinarily reluctant to prevent or put a stop to the recurrent genocides in Rwanda and Burundi. It is horrifying simply to record the numbers killed. Approximately 100,000 Tutsi were killed during the civil war in Rwanda in 1962–1963. Extremist Tutsi slaughtered a quarter of a million Hutu in Burundi in 1972.[5] About 100,000 people are estimated to have died in the fighting that broke out in Burundi after the assassination of President Ndadaye in 1993. During the latest genocide in Rwanda, the UN observer force already present in the country was not, at first, authorized to intervene on the grounds that this was a case of "tribal warfare."

---

4. De Waal would go even further and say that they are "in no sense *tribes* or even *ethnic groups*" (1994: 2).
5. This led the Carnegie Endowment for International Peace to put out a report excoriating the U.S. administration of President Nixon and Secretary of State Kissinger for its "indifference, inertia and irresponsibility" (see Leitenberg 1994: 33).

In fact, the Unitd Nations considered withdrawing its forces from Rwanda, but was shamed into keeping them there. It proved impossible, however, to send enough UN troops for them to have any decisive effect. The United States opposed sending troops to Rwanda. President Clinton stated that it was not in the national interest of the United States to send troops to help prevent the carnage and that the UN too should learn when to say "No" (Leitenberg 1994: 37). The harrowing story of international bickering over what to do (or whether to do anything at all) while the death toll mounted, is well told in Milton Leitenberg's essay (1994) on the effects of U.S. and UN actions in Rwanda. In the same essay he quotes the *New York Times* as reporting that, as the numbers of the dead mounted toward half a million, spokespeople for the United States were instructed not to refer to this as genocide because this would make the American policy of nonintervention more difficult to sustain (Leitenberg 1994: 38).

THE FORMER YUGOSLAVIA[6]

The other horror story that stunned the world in recent years is the grisly war in what used to be Yugoslavia, with all its accompanying atrocities (see map inside front cover). This war was all the more shocking because it occurred in Europe, and seemed to indicate that even the more advanced areas of the world are not immune from primordial hatreds that intermittently explode into savage warfare. In fact, the Balkans are generally assumed to be a region particularly prone to "tribal warfare." The very word *Balkanization* has come to stand for divisiveness and mutual hostility leading to separation into smaller and smaller national units. It has not always been so. The history of the region shows as much intermingling as conflict over the centuries.

The southwestern part of the Balkans that made up the territory of the former Yugoslavia was settled by tribes speaking Slavic languages who migrated into the region in the sixth and seventh centuries AD. This land of the southern Slavs (which is what *Yugoslavia* means in the Slavic languages) became a frontier zone between contending empires, religions, and civilizations. Its inhabitants were tugged this way and that, by Central European powers to the northwest, by Slavic powers to the northeast, and by the Ottomans to the southeast.

---

6. The account presented in this section is primarily drawn from Denitch 1994 and Hayden 1995. Other useful works to consult on the break-up of Yugoslavia are Djilas 1991 and Glenny 1992.

The Slovenes,[7] for example, were incorporated into Charlemagne's empire in the eighth century and remained firmly under the control of the Germanic successors to that empire until the break-up of Austria-Hungary at the end of the first world war.

The Croats also came under the influence of Charlemagne's empire at the beginning of the ninth century, but were able to keep a certain distance from it, retaining their independence in return for acknowledging the suzerainty of Charlemagne. In the tenth century, the Croats united with the Kingdom of Hungary, but after the Croats and Hungarians were defeated by the Turks in 1526, most of Croatia came under Turkish rule. Napoleon wrested Croatia from Turkey in 1809, but soon afterward (in 1813) Croatia became part of the Austro-Hungarian empire, in which it remained until the end of the first world war. As a result of their early contacts with the west, Slovenes and Croats adopted the Catholic form of Christianity rather than the eastern Orthodox form, which is the one commonly practiced by Serbs, Montenegrins, and Macedonians.

The Serbs, by contrast, adopted Orthodox Christianity in 879 but, nevertheless, fought to retain their independence from the waning Byzantine empire until the thirteenth century. They had their own state and were ruled by their own Tsar (emperor) until their catastrophic defeat by the Turks at the Battle of Kosovo in 1389. This heroic defeat, in which the Serbs chose death rather than surrender, has become a central theme in Serbian nationalism and in the Serbs's sense of themselves as staunch defenders of Christendom against the forces of Islam. They remained subject to the Turks until the nineteenth century, when their struggle for independence began in earnest. They succeeded in being recognized as an autonomous principality under Turkish suzerainty in 1829 and achieved full independence in 1878.

Further south, the Macedonian Slavs mingled with Greeks in the sixth and seventh centuries. Their region was incorporated into the Bulgarian empire in the ninth century. It was then ruled at different times by the Byzantine empire, by Bulgarians, and by Serbs until it was taken over by the Turks in the fourteenth century. At the Congress of Berlin in 1878, when the western powers carved up this region of the Balkans, they allocated part of it to the Austro-Hungarian empire (Slovenia, Croatia, and Bosnia-Herzegovina), recognized the independence of another part of it (Serbia and Montenegro), but left

---

7. See map inside back cover for the areas now corresponding to all the peoples discussed in this section.

Macedonia under Turkish control. In 1912, Greece and Serbia allied with Bulgaria to liberate Macedonia from Turkey. They succeeded in doing this but then promptly quarreled among themselves about the future of Macedonia. So, in 1913, Greece and Serbia went to war with Bulgaria to determine how that future should be decided. They did better in the fighting, with the result that southern Macedonia was incorporated into Greece, northern Macedonia into Serbia, and a smaller, eastern portion of it into Bulgaria.

Further west, the Montenegrins succeeded in using their difficult terrain and comparative inaccessibility to remain relatively independent. They were incorporated into the Serbian empire in the twelfth century, but they succeeded in maintaining their independence when Serbia was overrun by the Turks, and defended themselves successfully over the centuries against both Turks and Albanians.

Finally, the region of Bosnia-Herzegovina (henceforward referred to simply as Bosnia) was the most disputed territory of all. In the tenth century it was part of Serbia, then part of Croatia. In the eleventh century it came under Byzantine rule and was then taken over by Hungary. In 1386, it was conquered by Turkey as the Turks swept forward to overwhelm Serbia. After that, it became an important frontier province of the Ottoman empire, guarding against the Austro-Hungarians to the northwest. The Congress of Berlin assigned Bosnia to the Austro-Hungarian empire, and the province was fully incorporated into that empire in the early twentieth century.

It has often been assumed that it is the fault lines through this part of the Balkans that have set their inhabitants against each other. According to this view, Slovenes and Croats were Catholics who had been in the Austro-Hungarian empire on the western side of the civilizational divide. Bosnian Muslims still clung to the faith to which they had converted under the Ottoman Turks. Serbs were Orthodox Christians, who had been on the eastern side of the divide in the Ottoman empire until they broke free in the nineteenth century. These different histories and conflicting faiths were supposed to account for the hostilities that destroyed modern Yugoslavia.

This story, however, is simplistic to the point of distortion. Serbs, Croats, and Bosnians have not been on one side or the other of the imperial and civilizational divides. They have lived at the frontiers, making their accommodations with both sides and with each other. They have intermingled and intermarried for long periods. Nor are there other significant differences between these peoples. The majority of them (about 83 percent in the former Yugoslavia) spoke Serbian or Croatian, dialects of a single language that linguists commonly refer to as Serbo-Croatian. Slovene and Macedonian are distinct Slavic languages, but they are as closely related to Serbo-Croatian as, for example, Dutch is to German. The only significant populations of the former Yugoslavia who did not speak these Slavic languages were the Hungarians in the north, largely in Vojvodina and eastern Croatia, and the Albanians in the south, largely in Kosovo, southern Serbia, and western Macedonia (see Map 2).

At the beginning of the nineteenth century, Slovenes, Croats, and Bosnians were ruled by the Austro-Hungarian empire, and Serbs and Macedonians were ruled by the Ottomans. It was the Serbs who first broke free while the others continued their struggles for independence against their respective overlords. These Balkan demands for independence were convenient for the European powers at the beginning of the twentieth century because they were primarily directed against the Turks; but as nationalistic movements gathered strength in other places, the Balkan demands began to be viewed with some misgivings. The western powers realized that, if the principle of self-determination was to be generally accepted, it would threaten not only the Ottoman, but also the Austro-Hungarian and Russian empires. Russia was strongly supportive of the southern Slavs in their demand for independence, but ruled at the same time over plenty of peoples who were neither Russian nor Slavs. Britain and France likewise controlled overseas empires inhabited by a variety of peoples who might get it into their heads to demand self-determination. The Balkan independence movements were thus precursors of the freedom fighters who have, in the twentieth century, battled their colonial overlords until the European empires were dismantled.

The Turks were the first to be forced out of their European empire, but it was the defeat of Austria-Hungary in the first world war that made it possible to create a Kingdom of Serbs, Croats, and Slovenes that was renamed *Yugoslavia* in 1929. Yugoslavia brought together the closely related peoples of the southwestern Balkans for the first time in a single state. Serbia, which had fought on the side of the victorious allies in the war, expected to dominate the new nation because it had been independent itself for some time, and saw itself as having fought to liberate its fellow Slavs from Austro-Hungarian rule. The Croats, Slovenes, and Bosnian Muslims, newly released from the Austro-Hungarian empire, felt they were joining a voluntary federation of equal peoples who would together shape the nature of the new state of the southern Slavs. Meanwhile, the diehard nationalists among the southern Slavs, those who had been, for example, battling the Austro-Hungarian empire for Slovene or Croat independence, did not accept the new state of Yugoslavia at all, insisting that it also inhibited the right to self-determination of its constituent peoples.

The first Yugoslavia was held together during the interwar years (1919–1941) by Serbian hegemony imposed by a Serb royal family. This became a dictatorship in 1929, which created such opposition among the other constituent peoples that the monarchy reversed its course and began to allow more local autonomy than before. By 1939, Croatia had been granted such autonomy that it was virtually independent. In 1941, Yugoslavia was invaded and occupied by the Axis powers with tragic consequences, not only in terms of immediate suffering for the Yugoslavs, but also for the future of their nation.

The invaders dismantled Yugoslavia by lopping off pieces of it and giving them to neighboring states. Italy took territory in the northwest, Vojvodina was given to Hungary, and Macedonia to Bulgaria. The Germans occupied a now-reduced Serbia. Meanwhile, Bosnia was assigned to the puppet state of Croatia, which was to be governed by the Ustasa (the Croatian fascist party) under the tutelage of Germany and Italy.

The Ustasa government of Croatia intended to create a Croatia inhabited entirely by Croats. To do this, they planned, following Nazi theory and practice at that time, to eliminate all Jews and Gypsies in Croatia. Serbs would be treated differently. One-third of them would be killed; one-third of them would be driven out of Croatia (including Bosnia) altogether; and one-third would be converted from the Orthodox church to Catholicism, which would remove their national consciousness and thus, supposedly, de-Serbianize them.

Meanwhile, two main Serbian resistance groups took to the hills and battled both the occupiers and, eventually, each other. They were the Cetniks, who were Serbian royalists, and the Partisans, who were communists and enrolled people of all Yugoslavia's nationalities. Tito himself, who was a Partisan leader before he became president of Yugoslavia after the war, was a Croat. The Cetniks and the Partisans both fought the occupying powers but, as the war dragged on, they were increasingly drawn into a civil war against each other. The Partisans defeated the Cetniks in this war within a war, which enabled Tito, the Partisan leader, to establish his communist regime in post-war Yugoslavia.

The bitter memories of the killing and counter-killing that took place during the second world war are an important part of the hatreds that have flared up again recently and led to the break-up of Yugoslavia. It is difficult to know exactly who killed how many of whom, especially since all parties exaggerate their own losses and minimize their own responsibilities for political reasons. Bogdan Denitch has tried to examine the issue dispassionately (1994: 30–33). He concludes that about a million Yugoslavs lost their lives during the war. This is not so high a figure as it would be if one accepted all the claims as to how many people were killed in massacres, in death camps, or at the hands of the occupying forces or in the civil war that coincided with the end of the international conflict; but it is still a terrible toll, considering that the total population of Yugoslavia was only about 16 million at the time.

The worst massacres were carried out by the Ustasa regime in Croatia, directed largely against Serbs, but also against left-wing Croats, Jews, and Gypsies. The Ustasa maintained a notorious death camp at Jasenovac, where at least 100,000 Serbs met their death. The Germans and Austrians also massacred tens of thousands of civilians, mostly in Serbia, in reprisals against the resistance fighters. These, in their turn, were responsible for massacres too, although on a much lesser scale, because they did not have the power of the state behind them. Serbian Cetniks killed civilians in Bosnia, Montenegro, Croatia, and even Serbia itself. Finally, the victorious Partisans carried out mass executions of members of the Ustasa, of the Croat Home Guard, and of the Cetniks who were captured at the end of the war.

This was the troubled beginning of what some people have called the Second Yugoslavia. The reconstituted state was divided into six republics—Slovenia, Croatia, Serbia, Bosnia-Herzegovina (Bosnia), Montenegro, and Macedonia—together with two autonomous provinces—Vojvodina to the north of Serbia, with a large Hungarian minority, and Kosovo to the south of Serbia, populated mainly by Albanians. Although all of the republics (with the exception of Bosnia) were named for distinct peoples, these peoples had mingled with each other for centuries so it was impossible to separate Slovenes from Croats, from Serbs, from Muslims, and so on simply by drawing boundaries around where these groups lived. The internal boundaries of the regions of Yugoslavia known as Croatia, Bosnia, Serbia, and so on were never intended to be boundaries between peoples. On the contrary, the internal republics of Yugoslavia all contained large minorities. There were, for example, more than 650,000 Serbs in Croatia and about 1.3 million of them in Bosnia; just as there were about 200,000 Croats in Serbia and 800,000 in Bosnia. These peoples shared a common state when that state was Yugoslavia, albeit a state that was also common to the other peoples counted among the southern Slavs. It was the existence and the relatively successful functioning of that state that allowed the internal ethnic divisions to continue and even to be associated, at least in principle, with territories, without destabilizing the entire country.[8]

In fact, under Tito's communist regime, the country seemed to work well enough. Its people shared a sense of pride in the fact that they had accomplished their own liberation in the waning days of the second world war. They had welcomed the Red Army of the Soviet Union into Yugoslavia, not been liberated by it. In time they came to

---

8. Compare this to the "Spanish solution" discussed in the conclusion to Chapter 2.

feel that they were citizens of a unique country: European, communist, and not under the thumb of the Soviet Union. Even Yugoslav communism was *sui generis*. It had institutionalized self-management instead of centralized control. It permitted many Western-style freedoms, including the freedom to travel abroad, and succeeded in providing consumer goods for its citizens. Meanwhile, Tito was careful to ensure that all the constituent nationalities shared in the power of the republic, to dilute the otherwise probable domination of Serbia or Croatia. Yugoslavs could live where they wanted within Yugoslavia, even though the internal divisions of the country bore names corresponding to nationalities—with the exception of Bosnia. It was not until the census of 1971 that census forms gave Yugoslavs the option of describing themselves as Muslims instead of (say) Croats or Serbs, and subsequently the Muslims became the largest plurality of the population in Bosnia.

Although Tito tried to maintain some sort of balance among the constituent republics, he also insisted on one-party rule, and moved always to marginalize those who tried to liberalize and democratize the system. His preference was to maintain party control over the nation's life, but to make this palatable by transferring greater authority within the system to the internal republics. This served to undercut those who believed in Yugoslavia and worried about how to modernize both its society and its economy and bring it into line with the countries of Western Europe. Instead, it offered ample opportunities for people to play the ethnic card in their respective republics.

These opportunities were the dynamite that eventually blew up Yugoslavia. The country had profited from the availability of Western investment capital in the 1970s, but it was badly hit by the debt crisis that affected all "third world" borrower nations, to some degree, in the early 1980s. The economic downturn brought renewed criticism within Yugoslavia of the inefficient and bureaucratic way in which the economy was run, and also of the corruption and incompetence displayed by Communist managers.[9] All of these problems were highlighted by a scandal involving Agrokomerc, an agricultural enterprise that had transformed the area around Bihac in northern Bosnia into a modern center of food production and processing. It transpired that its director Fikret Abdic[10] had financed this develop-

---

9. This part of my account is drawn from Bette Denich's paper (forthcoming) entitled "Superfluity and Schismogenesis in the Dismantling of Yugoslavia."
10. This flamboyant character reappeared years later as the leader of a group of Muslims that did not accept the authority of the Muslim government in Sarajevo, obliging that government to take Bihac by force.

ment through a tangle of unsecured promissory notes. This "Agro-gate," as people began to call it, showed the dishonesty of Yugoslav managers and bank officials, left the banks carrying millions of dollars worth of debt, and showed that productivity in Yugoslavia was not rising as a result of the system, as had been officially claimed, but was being financed at a loss from abroad. Now that foreign lenders would no longer finance the Yugoslav economy, it became imperative to change the way the political system worked in order to modernize the economy and enable Yugoslavia to take its place among the prosperous nations of Western Europe.

Apart from putting an end to the incompetence and corruption rampant in the Titoist version of Communism, there was no agreement on what else needed to be done. Worse still, under decentralization within the Titoist system, the party leadership of each republic controlled the media there, so that different and opposing diagnoses of the Yugoslav malaise were being pronounced in the various republics. Slovenia and Croatia, the most economically developed republics, resented the Titoist system of taxing them to provide investment capital for the less-developed ones. They felt themselves to be the most "western" and "European" segments of an otherwise "backward" nation that acted as a drag on their economic progress. Serbia and Montenegro saw the situation differently. They felt that the fault lay with the neocolonial fashion in which Slovenia in particular acquired cheap labor and raw materials from the rest of Yugoslavia to fuel its own economic development, which in turn was assisted by its privileged access to the Yugoslav market. The root of the problem, in this analysis, was patronage and incompetence among the party managers (mostly not Serbs) at the highest levels of the nation. As Bette Denich points out, the media in each republic reported only its own version of its grievances without mentioning the contrary views held by others, so that a divide in public opinion opened up between the inhabitants of the prosperous republics in the north and those of the less-prosperous ones further south.

It was no accident that Slobodan Milosevic, who had been a party functionary all his life, took over the leadership of the Serbian communist party, at the head of a reformist faction, soon after the Agrokomerc scandal broke. He promised to replace incompetent party hacks with progressive managers who would really modernize the economy. More important, however, in his rise to power was his appeal to traditional Serbian nationalism. Kosovo, touching the southwestern edge of Serbia, was the site of Serbian heroism and their epic defeat by the Turks. The majority of the inhabitants of that province are today Albanian and they demanded greater autonomy. Milosevic replied by mobilizing Serb public opinion not only against Kosovo, but also against any other republic that thought there was justice in the Albanian demands to be treated as prescribed by the laws of Yugoslavia. He then succeeded in toppling the governments of Kosovo, Vojvodina, and Montenegro and replacing them with his allies. This destabilized the formal structure of the Yugoslav state, which had, since Tito's death, been run by a collective presidency of eight members, one each from the six republics and the two provinces. Serbia now controlled four of those votes and could thus block any measure of which it disapproved.

As Bogdan Denitch makes clear (1994: 56–61), there is a sad chain of causality connecting Tito's decision to decentralize rather than democratize in the 1970s with subsequent events in Yugoslavia. In the early 1970s Tito cracked down, not only on the extreme nationalists in Croatia, but also on the liberal and reformist Communist leaders of Slovenia, Serbia, and Macedonia. The latter were ousted from office and, in this way, Tito eliminated from political life the generation of leaders who were able and willing to cooperate with each other on the national level, regardless of ethnic differences. Tito thus disheartened the moderates and democrats throughout Yugoslavia. By trying to reform the system through decentralization rather than democratization, he undercut those who believed in Yugoslavia, and strengthened the communists-turned-nationalists who emerged as leaders in the individual republics.

When the Albanians felt that decentralization should involve giving them the local autonomy in Kosovo that other peoples enjoyed in other parts of Yugoslavia, Milosevic used this as a pretext to awaken Serbian nationalism and to increase Serbia's power within the federation. This coincided with multiparty elections in the other republics and contributed to the victories of nationalist parties, who claimed that theirs was the only way to stand up to Serbian expansionism. This, in turn, provoked quite reasonable fears among all Yugoslavs who lived outside of their own "ethnic republics" about what would happen to minorities if Yugoslavia should break up into separate republics governed by ethnic nationalist regimes.

At this stage there was probably no way to save the Yugoslav federation, but two subsequent events guaranteed that its break-up would be bitter and bloody. First, Slovenia and Croatia decided to secede and form independent states. The nations of the European Community were exceedingly reluctant to offer them immediate recognition, feeling that to do so without prior discussion of arrangements for the dissolution of Yugoslavia and guarantees for minorities within the new republics would probably result in war. Germany, however, insisted and the European Community, in order to maintain its unanimity, concurred. Second, the newly independent Republic of Croatia readopted symbols of the fascist Croatia, set up during World War II, and made it clear that it was to be a republic of

Croats where Serbs were unwelcome. The Serbs in Croatia rebelled against the Croatian government and Serbs and Croats went to war with each other, in Croatia and elsewhere.

This put intolerable pressure on Bosnia, which had not been involved in the previous events but was unwilling to remain in a Yugoslavia which was increasingly beginning to look like Greater Serbia. In early 1992, Bosnia took a referendum on independence. The Serbs in Bosnia boycotted the vote, but the rest of the population, including Bosnian Croats, gave it overwhelming support. Bosnia declared its independence and was immediately recognized by the United Nations, but the fighting was already spreading. Ironically, it was this republic—where relations between Serbs, Croats, and Muslims had been the most peaceful and that still insisted that its people, if left to themselves, could all get along—that was now being torn apart by ethnic extremists from Serbia and Croatia. There still are Serbs and Croats who want to be Bosnians and who actually fight alongside the Muslims to defend Bosnia, but the inexorable logic of the unfolding situation has made the Bosnian option an increasingly unattractive one for Serbs and Croats living there. Bosnia is under the constant threat of being divided between Croatia and Serbia, which would make it a safer bet for Serbs and Croats to go with the majorities in those countries rather then to side with a weak multiethnic state that may cease to exist and in which they would be minorities anyway.

Meanwhile, the war in Bosnia dragged on. The military advantage lay with the Serbs, who were supported by the Yugoslav army, which had become a Serbian rather than a federal force. The international community further tilted the balance toward Serbia without meaning to when it imposed an arms embargo on all the combatants. That left the Serbs with the weaponry of the Yugoslav army while their opponents were desperately smuggling in arms to build up their own forces. This was also a war that was characterized by *ethnic cleansing*. This sinister phrase referred to the practice of massacring people of a different ethnic group in order to clear their territory for settlement by their attackers.

The international community attempted to mediate and broker peace accords, but these efforts were, for a long time, unsuccessful. It was common knowledge that both the United Nations and the North Atlantic Treaty Organization disagreed over what to do, and the Russians strongly supported the Serbs, even when they carried out the most egregious massacres. The result was that when peacekeepers were sent, they were not backed up with sufficient force to enable them to intervene effectively, becoming virtual hostages of the forces that they were supposed to be restraining. This was nowhere more clearly demonstrated than in the town of Srebrenica in Bosnia, whose Muslim inhabitants were "protected" by a force of Dutch peacekeepers. The town was overrun by Bosnian Serbs, who took away hundreds of Muslim men in spite of the objections of the peacekeepers, and massacred them in a nearby field.

Srebrenica became the symbol of ethnic cleansing, a horrid reminder of the barbarities being carried out in the Yugoslav conflict and a wake-up call to the world in general and to the Europeans in particular. However, Slobodan Milosevic, as we have noted, had established himself as the voice of Serbian nationalism. He proved to be a wily negotiator for the Serbs, yet his negotiations, which bought time and prolonged suffering, were ultimately unsuccessful. He failed to keep Slovenia and Croatia in Yugoslavia by force, but invaded Croatia while supporting the Serbs in Bosnia. In 1995, a Croatian offensive drove Serbian troops out of their republic and prompted a mass exodus of Serbs from parts of Croatia they had occupied for centuries. Later, in 1995, Milosevic negotiated the Dayton accords, which formally turned Bosnia into a federation of Croats, Muslims, and Serbs; but this federation soon split into two separate territories, one run by Muslims and Croats and the other run by Serbs. Finally, Milosevic provoked yet another conflict in Kosovo, which led to his defeat and downfall.

I noted earlier that the majority of Kosovo's population is Albanian but because it is the symbolic locus of Serbian nationalism, the Serbian minority ruled despotically over the Albanian majority. When the Albanian Kosovars demanded their rights, they were suppressed. This led to a situation where the Albanians in Kosovo were divided into two factions, one demanding autonomy within Yugoslavia and the other demanding independence from Yugoslavia. When the Serbs sent in the army to impose Serb rule and the army began to carry out ethnic cleansing, forcing Albanian Kosovars from their homes and over the border as refugees, NATO intervened. NATO planes bombed the Yugoslav army and, more importantly, bombed Serbia, destroying much of its infrastructure. Yugoslavia capitulated and Kosovo was occupied by peacekeeping forces drawn from the NATO countries and Russia. This finally united the Serbian opponents of Milosevic. They were outraged by the wars into which Milosevic had led them, all of which they had lost. They were dismayed by the damage that NATO warplanes had inflicted on Serbia and by the corruption of Milosevic and his cronies, who managed to thrive in a collapsing economy that was reducing most Serbs to poverty. Milosevic clung on as long as he could, but was finally voted out of power in Yugoslavia and, later, in Serbia too. Milosevic was by no means the only ethnic entrepreneur who fished in the troubled waters of the former Yugoslavia, but he was certainly the most influential and, as a result, the most harmful. He was not only the prime mover in a whole series of wars that caused untold suffering to the civilian populations of Yugoslavia, but he was also the politician that had the most to do with the break-up of Yugoslavia and the defeat and impoverishment of Serbia.

CONCLUSION

The above discussion indicates that the supposedly "primordial" conflicts that led to genocide in Rwanda and ethnic cleansing and genocide in the former Yugoslavia, were not really primordial at all. It was the Europeans in Rwanda and Burundi who essentially separated Tutsi and Hutu into racial groups and then set them against each other. Other nations were later willing to intervene in Tutsi–Hutu disputes, supporting one side or the other, but the international community did not put its weight behind those in Rwanda and Burundi who wanted to solve the disputes by reconciling the warring parties, nor did it make much effort to forestall or curtail the genocidal slaughters that took place.

Similarly, the intractable ethnic hatreds that were assumed to lie behind the conflict in the former Yugoslavia turned out to have been more created than innate. It was assumed that the fault lines through this part of the Balkans had set its inhabitants against each other. Yet, we saw that Serbs, Croats, and Bosnians have lived at the frontiers of these divisions and have intermingled for centuries. The rise of nationalism in the nineteenth century fueled their struggles for independence and gave them a keener sense of separateness from each other than they had had in the past. The seeds of bitterness that have recently borne such hideous fruit were, however, planted during the second world war when Yugoslavia was dismembered by foreign powers, its peoples deliberately set against each other, and the country plunged into an orgy of killing and counter-killing. Those memories were sternly put aside in Tito's Yugoslavia, and might have been allowed to fade if there had been more time and better political preparation for the Yugoslav idea to catch on. But Yugoslavia at the end of the 1980s faced a crisis similar to the one that broke up the Soviet Union. An economic crisis, together with a feeling that things were not working well anymore, produced a nationwide malaise. People did not know where to turn and Tito, like the Soviet leaders, had prevented the emergence of robust civil institutions within the country. It was a situation that provided ample opportunities for ethnic entrepreneurs, and this was the guise in which old party functionaries, like Tudjman in Croatia and Milosevic in Serbia, reincarnated themselves.

Even at this stage, with the constituent units of the former Yugoslavia defining themselves ethnically,[11] it might have been possible for the country to break up without the fighting and atrocities that actually took place. The unilateral declarations of independence by individual republics, without any agreements with the others about how issues of common interest, especially the rights of minorities in each other's territories, were to be handled, made a peaceful separation exceedingly unlikely. The speedy recognition of these breakaway republics by the European Community, at German insistence, made war inevitable.

It is sometimes thought that the very centrality of interethnic issues is enough to condemn a society to instability and even violence. This is another one of the conventional explanations advanced for the massacres in Rwanda and the former Yugoslavia. Once again, the explanation is wrong. The existence of ethnic groups and ethnic distinctions do not of themselves create ethnic conflict. In the genocidal situations we have just examined, ethnic hostility was to some extent created and certainly inflamed in those countries by the intrusive actions of outside powers. Some people would go so far as to say that tribalism in Africa was a creation of the colonial papers. This is an exaggeration, but it is certainly true that the groups that might have been considered tribes in pre-colonial times were changed and reshaped by colonial policies and pressures. The example of the Tutsi and the Hutu in Rwanda and Burundi is an extreme case of such colonial manipulation and does come close to representing a colonialist creation of tribal identities.

If external forces created the ethnic hostility in these cases, it was internal ethnic entrepreneurs who took advantage of it in order to advance their own power and political agendas. The third ingredient of these horrifying genocides was international incomprehension and neglect. The incomprehension is difficult to understand, for these were virtually paradigmatic cases of genocide that should not have taken the world by surprise. The failure to understand what was happening and why until it was too late was due to the tendency to interpret and write off such horrors as being the result of age-old ethnic conflicts. This tendency, in its turn, excused inaction and made a virtue out of "not getting involved."

---

11. With the exception of Bosnia, which remains staunchly committed to multiethnicity within its own domain. Unfortunately, only some Croats and Serbs in Bosnia share this multiethnic conviction. Many, if not most of them, prefer (or regard it as more prudent) to stick with the Croats of Croatia and the Serbs of Serbia.

Another feature that is widely present in situations of ethnic hostility is the ethnic definition of the state. The devastating consequences of defining the state as the domain of a single ethnic group are all too well known. The result is not, as optimists might imagine, that every ethnic group gets its own state. On the contrary, because the vast majority of states in the world are multiethnic, each state becomes the province of a dominant ethnic group, which then has the right to define others as outsiders, expel them if necessary, or, in extreme cases, eliminate them physically.

All of these features were present when the former Yugoslavia broke up. First, there was the violent intrusion of outside powers that came to a head in the second world war. Second, there was an increasing tendency to define the internal republics of the country in ethnic terms. Third, high officials of the now-discredited communist party adopted the new guise of ethnonationalist leaders in these republics. Fourth, these ethnic entrepreneurs received support from the peoples of the internal republics, who were shocked and bewildered by the disintegration of their expectations at a time of political chaos and economic collapse. Finally, external powers once again intervened to hasten the break-up of the country on the worst possible terms.

A similar scenario is being played out in the former Soviet Union. There, the republics of which the nation was formally comprised were always defined ethnically, though this was largely for show under Stalin. Now the ethnonationalism, which was intended to be ornamental in Stalin's day, has been reactivated, often, as in Yugoslavia, by old communists reincarnated as new nationalists. Hobsbawm's remark about the peoples of Central and Eastern Europe applies equally well to the peoples of the former Soviet Union. They will, he wrote: "...go on living in countries disappointed in their past, probably largely disappointed with their present, and uncertain about their future. This is a very dangerous situation. People will look for someone to blame for their failures and insecurities. The movements and ideologies most likely to benefit from this mood are...likely to be movements inspired by xenophobic nationalism and intolerance. The easiest thing is always to blame strangers" (Hobsbawm 1993: 62).

These situations bear an uncomfortable similarity to what happened in Germany after the first world war, where defeat and economic collapse contributed to the nation's willingness to listen to an earlier ethnic entrepreneur. Adolf Hitler played with the fires of German nationalism and racial superiority and made a scapegoat of Jews and Gypsies, resulting in genocide and war on an unparalleled scale.

The comparison with Hitler brings out another aspect of ethnonationalism. It is not only whipped up by ethnic entrepreneurs, but the main technique used by the latter is the manipulation of discourse and the creation of meaning. Hitler was a mesmeric speaker who success-fully persuaded the majority of the German people to accept a view of the world that saw Germany's defeat in the first world war as a tempo-rary setback caused largely by traitors. He persuaded them that the German destiny was to rule over lesser races and to start by gathering all Germans into a single state, which would be cleansed of undesir-able populations. Germany was to be made, in his sinister terminology, *Judenrein*, literally "clean of Jews."

This raises the troubling question of how modern nations can deal with inflammatory discourse of the kind that Hitler used so ef-fectively, and that is still the principal weapon of ethnonationalist leaders to this day. Modern Germany has made hate speech, particu-larly any speech that glorifies Nazism, illegal. Indonesia, likewise, has not hesitated to ban speech calculated to promote ethnic strife. This measure, however effective it may have been in Indonesia, is un-likely to appeal to democratic countries that will not tolerate the de-gree of authoritarianism wielded by the Indonesian regime, and that deeply value a tradition of free speech.

There is, however, something to be learned from Indonesia's han-dling of ethnicity. Above all, it is a country that has admitted its eth-nic diversity and set out consciously and systematically to treat it as a resource and a source of pride rather than a disaster waiting to hap-pen. The Indonesian motto of "Unity in Diversity" might at first seem to indicate much the same thing as the motto of the United States, "E Pluribus Unum," but there is an important difference be-tween the two concepts. The Indonesian notion is timeless and points to the fact there will always be diversity in Indonesia and that this di-versity supplies the ingredients for Indonesian unity. The U.S. motto, in contrast, refers to a process, indicating that the United States will take the many and meld them into one. The Indonesian ideology ac-cepts the permanence of ethnic diversity; the U.S. one does not. They both represent quite different views of the role of ethnicity within the nation and the way it should be dealt with. The Indonesian view is that it should be accommodated and given a permanent, but nondi-visive place within the system. The U.S. view is that people are wel-come to bring their ethnic attitudes and behaviors to the United States with them, but they are expected to tone them down as they adapt to the common civic culture of the United States.

The example of Spain shows that it is not necessary to have an au-thoritarian regime in order to make concessions to ethnicity within the nation. In fact, the Spanish tendency has been just the opposite. Spain's authoritarian regimes have, in recent times, been the ones that tried to suppress ethnic and regional autonomy in the name of national unity. It is the democratic ones that have arranged for local autonomy to allow different "nationalities" and regionalisms to func-tion as part of the system rather than undermining it.

Spain faces two diametrically opposed kinds of problems at this moment. If the conservatives return to power and try to curtail the regional autonomy that has been so painstakingly built into the system, it may provoke renewed ethnic conflict. If, on the other hand, the present regionalism is allowed to continue, it may produce centrifugal tendencies within Spain itself. Catalonia especially tends to feel that it is an industrially advanced region that is being "held back" by the "backward areas" of the country, much as Slovenia felt in the former Yugoslavia.

The point to note, however, is not that Indonesia or Spain or any other country can solve all its problems by dealing with its ethnic issues. What such examples do show is that ethnicity need not be destabilizing if it is accommodated within the arrangements made by the state. Furthermore, if it can be so accommodated, this is of incalculable advantage, for other problems that may arise do not get transposed into ethnic issues that, as we have seen, are peculiarly divisive.

It is exceedingly difficult in most societies—but not impossible—to prevent divisive issues from becoming issues of ethnic conflict. This is not because ethnicity is some kind of instinct that leads human beings to bond with their own and fight outsiders. Rather, ethnicity is a latent qualification for membership in a group that every human possesses and that may be activated under certain circumstances. The problem is that those circumstances are often conflictive ones. In fact, anthropologists have referred to ethnicity as "an ascriptive mask of confrontation" (Vincent 1974: 399) or as a "reservoir for turbulence in a world where power, wealth, and dignity are unevenly and illegitimately distributed within and among nations" (Nash 1989: 127). Ethnicity is thus activated when human beings are under stress. Its potential does not go away and it is difficult or impossible to suppress without genocide. It follows that the best way to deal with it is to acknowledge it and make room for it within states. This, too, is extremely hard to do for the reasons mentioned above by Nash, to which I would add other, equally powerful ones. It is especially hard to do when states are willing, as a matter of policy, to stir up ethnic conflicts in other states or when unscrupulous political leaders within states are willing to play the ethnic card to advance their personal or group ambitions. That is why the search for multi-ethnic solutions is so critical and why it is important to learn from those countries that have sought to accommodate ethnicity in order to avoid ethnic conflict.

4

The State

STATE AND NATION

We live in a world of states. They make the rules according to which we live our lives and provide us with an important part of our identities. It is hard to imagine how "stateless" people can manage in such a world. They are invariably those who are afflicted in some way—refugees or people whose state has been obliterated by some international cataclysm, outcasts in any case, people who seem to have no place in normal human society. The state seems to be such an essential feature of human organization that it is difficult to remember that it is a comparatively recent development.

In medieval Europe, people did not think of themselves as belonging to this or that state, but rather as serving this or that lord, and the lords themselves were part of a complex mosaic of overlapping jurisdictions, involving pope and emperor, princes and feudal lords, guilds and vested interests. The very word for the state in its modern sense was first introduced into the vocabulary of politics by Machiavelli in the sixteenth century. It was not until the seventeenth century that the essential idea of the state began to be generally accepted, namely that there should be a single, supreme authority over a group of people occupying a common territory.[1] That authority, in those days, was invariably an absolute monarch.

Thomas Hobbes, writing in seventeenth century England, justified this rule in his famous book *Leviathan* (1651), where he argued that man would naturally wish to bind himself into a commonwealth with other men, in order to avoid that state of war of all against all in

---

1. This is, obviously, a minimal definition of the state. Another defining characteristic of the state, emphasized by Max Weber, is that it has a monopoly over the legitimate use of physical force.

which life, to use his powerful and much-quoted phrase, would be "nasty, brutish and short." The only way for human beings to ensure that those within the commonwealth do not revert to the war of all against all is for them to create a mortal God (the Leviathan) who governs them and mediates between them and the one Supreme God. This Leviathan is the sovereign. The absolute monarch rescues his subjects from the Hobbesian nightmare world in which every man is out for himself and pitted against every other man. In return, his subjects must submit to the dictates of the sovereign, who embodies the principle of order.

Of all the seventeenth and eighteenth century thinkers who came to be known as the philosophers of the enlightenment, Hobbes offered perhaps the most authoritarian view of the social contract that binds humans together in society. Yet the very idea of society as a social contract rather than a divinely ordained state of affairs led to reformist and eventually revolutionary thinking about the state. The maintenance of law and order came to be considered insufficient justification for a ruler. Subjects were considered to have rights too, and could hope for and even demand a state that tried to ensure such things as social justice and human happiness. Rousseau, for example, writing in *The Social Contract* (1762), insisted that sovereignty was an inalienable right of the people and that government was only legitimate in so far as it reflected the "general will" of the people themselves. These views got him into trouble in France, and he had to go into exile in Switzerland.

These ideas about the state all grappled with the problem of order, of the responsibilities of rulers and the rights of the ruled; but even the revolutionary theories of the state did not deal with the question of what happens when the ruled are not a homogenous group. This was because the ideas that led up to the American and French revolutions stressed the rights of individuals. People were no longer to be considered subjects of a ruler but citizens of a state. Furthermore, as Rousseau had argued in *The Social Contract*, they would enjoy equality before the state, which would in turn treat them uniformly. These were the ideas, summed up in the French revolutionary slogan of "liberty, equality and fraternity," that informed the liberal vision of the state, a vision that saw the state as deriving its legitimacy from the people and as catering to the people as equal individuals.

One of the few thinkers of the late eighteenth century who did worry about diversity and divisions among the citizens themselves was James Madison. In the *Federalist Paper (Number 10)* (1787), he focused on the problem of "factions." In small republics, he suggested, a faction could establish tyranny. In a large one, competing factions could undermine the state. The remedy for this was to create a large and diverse republic in which no one faction has the power to desta-bilize it. Madison was worrying mainly about religious differences, which he perceived as the main source of political factionalism, but his argument stressed the virtues of a kind of pluralism or at least of balanced diversity among the citizenry.[2]

The French revolutionary concept of the state, on the other hand, stressed its rationality and homogeneity; not because France itself was a homogenous society at that time—most of its citizens did not even speak French—but because citizenship was conferred on all those who accepted the laws, liberties, and responsibilities of France, which included speaking or learning to speak French (Hobsbawm 1990: 21). German thinkers at the beginning of the nineteenth century were less convinced of the merits and rationality of the state and more concerned with the problem of the nation. Germans were, after all, scattered throughout northern and central Europe in many differ-ent states and petty principalities. Yet leading German writers in-sisted that there was something—and something valuable—that all Germans had in common. It was not just their language, but also the spirit of their people or, as we would now say, their culture. The problem was that there was no state that acted as a vehicle for this culture. Herder, writing in 1800, was an ardent proponent of the idea that every people, not just the Germans, had its own spirit so that the task of the historians[3] became that of understanding their particular spirit. He was less optimistic about humanity's progress toward a ra-tional state, for he noted that states were, as often as not, artificial so-cial formations created through the conquest and distortion of nations. It was nations that allowed the expression of all that was best in humankind.

It is true that many Francophile Germans welcomed the French revolution and even the Napoleonic conquests of German lands, be-lieving this to be the wave of the future; but disillusion with the con-quering French soon set in. The whole experience had meanwhile stoked the fires of German nationalism. By 1808, writers like Fichte were urging the Germans to come together and collaborate in the full flowering of German culture. This German state would set an exam-ple to the world because of the merits of its German-ness not, as in the French case, because the new state was held to be the most

---

2. Madison's concerns were not necessarily shared by the other authors of the Federalist Papers. John Jay, for example, was at pains to stress that the United States was fortunate because of the homogeneity of its population, a homogeneity that he exaggerated.

3. And, he might have added, of anthropologists and other social scientists.

advanced embodiment of rationality and progress. Above all, the German state would be the expression of the German nation.

What, then, is a nation as distinct from a state? It is easier to start by saying what it is not. Nations are not natural units to which human beings automatically belong. Rather, they are units created by feelings of nationalism.[4] People have to come to feel that, for whatever reason, they are members of a nation for that nation to exist. A linguist cannot, for example, create a nation by identifying a group of people who share a distinct language and the oral and written traditions that are expressed in it; but the work of linguists in the nineteenth century often inspired people to start thinking of themselves as a nation, where they had not done so before. To think of one's group as constituting a nation is to think of it as a potential state. A state may and, as we have seen, more often than not does contain many subgroups. We have dealt in this book specifically with ethnic groups. Every ethnic group shares a common culture, a sense of common history and of its own distinctiveness. This is the essence of the nation or of what German speakers call the *Volk*. Such a people only becomes a nation in the technical sense if it thinks of itself as a potential state. Nationalism, then, is the notion that the nation and the state should coincide.

The nineteenth and twentieth centuries have seen a great upsurge of nationalism, first in Europe and later in other parts of the world, as the subjects of the old empires demanded their independence. Theorists of nationalism in the nineteenth century felt strongly, however, that not all nations could or should aspire to be states. Some were simply too small and would therefore be better off if they allowed themselves to be absorbed by the states that encompassed them. As John Stuart Mill put it in a vivid and often quoted passage:

> Nobody can suppose that it is not more beneficial to a Breton, or a Basque of French Navarre, to be brought into the current of the ideas and feelings of a highly civilized and cultivated people—to be a member of the French nationality, admitted on equal terms to all the privileges of French citizenship, sharing the advantages of French protection, and the dignity and prestige of French power—than to sulk on his own rocks, the half savage relic of past times, revolving in his own mental orbit, without participation or interest in the general movement of the world. The same remark applies to the Welshman or the Scottish Highlander as members of the British nation. (Mill 1861/1951: 490)

---

4. See Gellner 1983: 48–49 and Hobsbawm 1990: 10–11.

Those nationalists who advocated independence for peoples too small to become viable states were accused of what German-speakers aptly called *Kleinstaaterei* (Small-state-ism) and thought to be people who were not serious about the stability of the international order. At the same time, it is interesting to note that the nineteenth century theorists saw only two possibilities for small peoples and cultures that did not have their own states. The first was to aspire to statehood, but that was undesirable *Kleinstaaterei;* the second, and only real option, was to evaporate into the mainstream. A third possibility, that of limited autonomy within a multicultural state, was not given serious consideration. The existence of multinational states was recognized, as it had to be, simply because so many states were just that, with people of different ethnicities inextricably mingled within them, but it was assumed that the smaller nationalities would in the end be absorbed by the larger ones to their mutual benefit.

A nation, as defined here, is related to but clearly different from a state. This is bound to cause confusion because, in colloquial English, we tend to use the words interchangeably. In fact the adjective commonly used in English to refer to things of the state is *national,* so *national defense* refers to the defense of the realm as a whole, even when the realm may contain separate ethnic groups or "nations." The confusion is perpetuated in the title of our world organization—the *United Nations.* Technically, it should really be called the *United States,* but that would further compound the confusion. In fact, a play on precisely this confusion became an issue between the United States and the USSR at the time of the founding of the United Nations. Stalin argued that, because the Soviet Union was a union of autonomous republics, each of the republics should be given a seat and a vote in the new world body. Truman countered by threatening to demand a seat and a vote for every state within the United States. The compromise reached was to seat Belarus and Ukraine as well as the USSR. It is ironic that Stalin's demand has finally been accepted but only after the collapse of the USSR and the recognition of its republics as independent states.

The technical distinction between state and nation is critically important, however, because so many of the world's problems involve the lack of correspondence between the two. The USSR used to have a "nationalities policy" designed by Stalin himself, according to which each major nationality of the former Soviet Union had its own autonomous republic. Since the republics were not really autonomous and the state was controlled from Moscow largely by Russians, the problems of the USSR were not seen as ethnic problems. Now that the autonomous republics have become independent states, each controlled by its dominant nationality and each containing significant minorities (sometimes Russian minorities), the former Soviet Union is riven with ethnic disputes.

As we saw in Chapter 2, the Chinese language does not distinguish between the nation (at the level of the state), a nationality (as part of the state), a people, or an ethnic group. Furthermore, the Chinese concept of nationality resembles the French concept discussed previously in that it does not depend on the coming together of people who already have some kind of ethnicity in common. People are considered Chinese in perpetuity if they have ever belonged to the Chinese family of nations. Since this family is dominated numerically and politically by Han Chinese, a cynic would interpret the Chinese theory as insisting, in effect, that peoples once conquered by the Han must always remain under Han domination. The Chinese, on the other hand, argue that it is not so much a matter of domination as of civilization. Those who have been brought into the orbit of Han civilization cannot leave it, for they become part of it.

The central issue here is the relationship between the state, as it is politically defined, and its constituent nations. I use the plural here deliberately, for most states in the world today contain a number of different peoples, yet we often speak of such states as *nation-states,* implying that the state corresponds to a single nation. The United Nations, for example, as an organization of member states, is solicitous of the rights of states, for it is on a proper respect for these that our present world order is constructed. It has also, since its founding, gone on record as being concerned about the rights of individuals and how to protect them (usually against the state). It has, however, only recently and hesitantly begun to pay formal attention to the rights of peoples (or nations as we might call them[5]) who do not control states.

It is easy, as a practical matter, to see why this should be so, but I believe that such hesitancy is not solely due to practicality. It is, I think, very much part of the political theoretical tendency, at least in the west, to assume that nation building is the same thing (or ought to be) as strengthening the state. Not, of course, strengthening the state in the sense of establishing dictatorship, but rather strengthening democratic states so that they can function efficiently and well, unencumbered by ethnic divisiveness—in effect, following the French revolutionary lead and treating ethnicity as if it will soon evaporate, rather than the thinking of the German writers who focused on the relationship between ethnicity and the state.

Again, this is understandable. What I am here calling the French tradition, although it was shared, in whole or in part, by many think-

---

5. And as Native Canadians do when they refer to themselves as members of Canada's First Nations.

ers in other countries (particularly in the United States), focused on a theory of the state that could guarantee freedom, equality, and democracy to its citizens. It is a preoccupation that is at the heart of what we commonly think of as *Western Civilization.* Furthermore, it is based on the optimistic notion, characteristic of the spirit of the enlightenment, that as such states develop and flourish, their citizens will also become more reasonable and rational and will abandon their traditional ethnic attachments. Improvement of the state will thus cause ethnicity to vanish. By contrast, the German theoretical concern with peoples and their cultures and how to accommodate these to the state was seen as a conservative tendency harking back to the very ethnicity that would cease to exist in a truly modern state. It was a theory that assumed these cultures would continue to exist in spite of modernization. Worse still, it actually glorified them and found merit in the particularities of different traditions rather than focusing on the advantages that would accrue to all, once those separatist traditions had become obsolete.

Furthermore, this focus on peoples and their rights rather than on states and their advantages has had devastating consequences in our present century. The suppressed nationalisms of southeastern Europe supplied the tinder that eventually blazed up in the conflagration of the first world war. At the end of that war, a serious effort was made to defuse these national tensions by allowing some of the suppressed nationalities to form their own independent states. President Wilson, who led this effort, felt it was only logical that those who believed in democracy should support the cause of freedom for *peoples* as well as for *people.* Unfortunately, the effort ended in failure. It was not politically or practically possible to allow every people with a sense of nationalism to form its own state. The map of Europe was redrawn, permitting the Czechs and the Slovaks to form the new state of Czechoslovakia, the Southern Slavs to form Yugoslavia, and so on. Inevitably, though, most states, including the new ones, still retained substantial minorities within their borders who were not of the dominant nationality or nationalities. These were often minorities who were also glowing with the prevailing spirit of nationalism and who felt neglected when their particular nationalistic aspirations could not be met. The League of Nations was supposed to offer protection to minorities, but it proved incapable of doing that. Worse still, it could not even protect states such as Czechoslovakia, which had cooperated with the League and tried to live up to its precepts by actually putting its protective policies toward minorities into practice.

Meanwhile, the issue of minority rights came to be cynically manipulated by powerful states, particularly by Nazi Germany. The Nazis gave a new twist to the appeals of Herder and Fichte. The latter had sought to unite all Germans so that together they could set an example of civilization. The Nazis also sought to unite all Germans, but for different reasons. They insisted that Germans, because they belonged to a superior race, should be united in the Nazi state, which would have the power to exercise its dominion over inferiors. This was their excuse for joining with Austria and dismembering Czechoslovakia, a series of actions that led to the outbreak of the second world war.

Given this grim history, it is understandable that arguments for minority rights and self-determination acquired a bad name and that the United Nations, even in the period of optimism immediately following the second world war, focused on the rights of individuals and the rights of states. Meanwhile, from the United Nations down, the casual equation of state and nation begs one of the most important questions of our times. It assumes that each state corresponds to a nation and thus ignores peoples or nations that do not control states.

IDEAL STATE AND REAL STATES

We are now in a position to answer the question posed in Chapter 2. Why was the study of ethnicity and the state comparatively neglected, especially when it now seems so obviously central to national and international affairs? The short answer is that ethnicity was, for a long time, considered both pernicious and obsolescent. Theorists of the modern state regarded ethnic attachments as archaic survivals that hindered the process of modernization. Orthodox Marxists regarded ethnicity as "false consciousness"—a mistaken ideology that masked the true realities of class distinction and class conflict. Either way, it was bound to disappear as it was rendered irrelevant by modernization or by the emergence of classless societies. It therefore made sense to focus on the needs of a truly modern state and the means necessary for developing it—or to concentrate on the strategy for setting up classless societies. If these ends could be achieved, and the optimists thought that they were at least within reach, then the problem of ethnicity would be solved because it would just evaporate.

For some time now these theories have been criticized as wishful thinking. Isaiah Berlin criticized the tendency of observers who believed in the liberal theory of the state to dismiss nationalism as a "passing phase" (1979). Lijphart summed up this critique when he wrote:

> The expectation of declining ethnic conflict in the Western world has probably also been furthered by the liberal ideal of equality combined with liberal optimism. The liberal principle that people should be treated as individuals and not as members of racial, religious or other groups, together

with the liberal faith in progress, contribute to an unrealistic view that in the most advanced liberal democracies in the world, membership in ethnic groups must become increasingly irrelevant. Actual developments show that it is easier to change discriminatory laws than discriminating, or merely self-differentiating attitudes." (1977: 53)

It gradually became apparent that these theories were poor predictors. Ethnicity and ethnic conflict were not disappearing, even in the most "advanced" countries. In fact, European states in the twentieth and twenty-first centuries have not on the whole been good examples of the values of the enlightenment. They have given the world fascism, nazism, stalinism, and a variety of other state systems relying on authoritarianism and intolerance, often ethnic intolerance. Even now, in Europe's current post-totalitarian period, it is by no means clear that current European states embody the principles that the enlightenment theorists hoped for. Apart from the ethnic cleansing that ravaged the former Yugoslavia, the major countries of Europe are plagued with anxiety about "outsiders" and are prone to outbreaks of discrimination and even violence against them. In Germany and France, the "outsiders" attacked have even included fellow citizens whose ethnic background differs from the mainstream.

How could one account for this? Either true modernization or really classless societies were much more difficult to achieve than had previously been thought, so that in the medium term we would all have to deal with ethnicity and its consequences; or, even worse, the theories were wrong, in which case neither modernization nor the abolition of class warfare would necessarily eliminate ethnic attachments. Either way, the bankruptcy of our traditional theories of ethnicity left us with few and unattractive theoretical or political options. When it could be reliably argued that ethnicity was about to disappear, it made a certain kind of sense to ignore it or suppress it. Now these arguments have proved hollow, and the world has woken up to the fact that ignoring or denying ethnicity will not work. It is now clear that the enlightenment ideal of the liberal state, so powerfully championed by the French and American revolutions, is not the inevitable and expectable culmination of modernization.[6]

---

6. Enloe 1973 makes an extended argument to this effect and points out how theorists of the state have systematically underestimated the power of ethnicity. Young 1993 surveys the growing awareness among political scientists of the shortcomings of their previous theorizing about ethnicity and the state.

Instead, it is an idea that was painfully and incompletely realized in certain European countries and their overseas offshoots, and, even in those countries, "retribalization" may be setting in, or so their newspapers seem to fear.[7] Meanwhile, it is also feared that the rest of the world was never effectively detribalized, so that "Balkanization," with all its frightening connotations, is not an aberration occurring in certain parts of the globe, but may very well be the normal state of affairs to be expected everywhere.

This is a gloomy scenario and it is small wonder that it provokes so much anxiety, for it is tantamount to saying: "We thought we knew what civilization was and how to achieve it, but we were wrong." I suggest, however, that this pessimism is as misguided as was the previous optimism about the imminent disappearance of ethnicity. The new pessimism seems to derive from jumping to premature conclusions about the nature and consequences of ethnic attachments, about the nature and needs of the state, and about the presumed incompatibility between them. It was presumed that we had a clear idea of what ethnicity was and that it would lead inevitably to tribalism, divisiveness, and, in extreme cases, separatism. Yet we have known for years that the cultural content of ethnicity is not uniform and that it does not always entail conflict. Similarly, we have been coming to realize, albeit more slowly, that ethnicity does not necessarily undermine the state, so that states have other options than stamping out all expressions of ethnic sentiment. The problem is that ethnic groups with strong nationalist feelings often *do* enter into conflict with each other and that states *are* from time to time torn apart by ethnic uprisings or interethnic wars.

ETHNICITY AND THE STATE RECONSIDERED

It is important to remember that neither a people's ethnicity nor the state (or states) in which this is expressed are static entities. They are both processes. Furthermore, they are processes that do much to define each other. That is why it is critical to understand both the history and context of ethnic affirmation or nationalism as well as the history and circumstances of the arena in which it acts, namely the state.

---

7. The press on both sides of the Atlantic reverts constantly to this theme—see for example *The Economist,* June 29, 1991—and it has received extended scholarly treatment in many places, notably in books by Peter Riesenberg (1992) and Arthur Schlesinger Jr. (1992).

The cases examined in Chapter 2 indicated conclusions about ethnicity that do not confirm the prevailing pessimism about its inevitably destabilizing effects. The peoples of Central Asia, inhabiting an area historically famous for sweeping conquests, nevertheless worked out a *modus vivendi* that enabled different peoples to live intermingled and with relatively little friction until the coming of Stalinism. It was Stalin's policy to give ethnic definitions to the soviet republics—a way of pretending to respect the autonomy of peoples within the former Soviet Union—while nevertheless keeping them, like everybody else, under firm control. When that control was removed and the republics of the former Soviet Union became independent, their ethnic definitions came to haunt them, especially because some of them are burdened with large and resentful Russian minorities who have no wish to assimilate and who cannot easily go home. It is no exaggeration to say that, in Central Asia, a working multiethnic system was destroyed and deliberately replaced by ethnic states.

Even the two worst-case scenarios, Rwanda and the former Yugoslavia, are not clear examples of the baleful effects of ethnicity. The sharp distinction between Tutsi and Hutu was artificially created, and they were separated into antagonistic pseudo-castes by colonial policies before they began to compete for control of their independent states. Similarly, the peoples who lived together in Yugoslavia had a long history of coexistence before they were torn apart by outside powers during the second world war. In fact, they coexisted again in the second Yugoslavia under Tito before they were once again torn apart by a combination of external influences and the internal effects of the opportunistic nationalism of their once-communist leaders. The most striking aspect of the tragic story of the Southern Slavs is the extent to which it has been constantly recast by powerful outsiders.

The counterexamples of Spain and Indonesia show that different peoples can coexist in the same state without ethnic conflict. These examples are hardly reassuring, however. Indonesia's "Unity in Diversity" seems to be badly frayed now that Suharto's dictatorship has given way to economic and poitical crisis. In fact, our examples seem to show that, although there is nothing primordial about ethnic conflict, there is a tendency for ethnic differences to persist over years or even centuries as possible contexts of conflict, to be invoked when societies are under stress. It is precisely this stress factor of dramatic changes taking place throughout the world that has provided the circumstances in which ethnic conflict has now broken out in so many places.

Thirty years ago, it seemed to serious analysts that the nation-state, for all its problems, was slowly but surely taking over the world. Now we appear to have entered a new era when, to quote the titles of two recent collections of essays, the nation-state is at bay or under siege.[8] Clearly, this new era is marked by the reconfiguration of world politics after the end of the cold war and the spectacular implosion of the Soviet Union.

The uncertainties of the post–cold war period have particularly affected countries that are remote from the centers of power. In the bipolar world of the cold war, when the West and the Communist bloc were locked in a perpetual and seemingly endless struggle, many of these countries were endowed with strategic significance. Their governments could count on aid and armaments from one side or the other. This made for a certain stability by strengthening the hand of those who controlled the state. If the state in question became a contested area, the superpowers would arm their local proxies to fight it out. Now that the cold war is over, many of the contested states have lost their strategic significance. The Horn of Africa, for example, was once contested by the superpowers, but is no longer, any more than Yemen or Angola. The legacy of the cold war era remains, however, in the form of large stocks of armaments that are used by today's factions to do battle with each other without superordinate control from the great powers. The recent civil war in Afghanistan was a classic example of this.

Other states, particularly in Africa and Asia, achieved their independence during the wave of decolonization that accompanied the disbanding of the European empires. Their boundaries were, therefore, colonial ones, representing lines of demarcation between the old imperial jurisdictions. Within those boundaries there were usually a variety of different peoples, often speaking different languages and having little in common with each other beyond the shared experience of colonial rule by a single occupying power. In Africa, the old colonial boundaries were by mutual agreement retained and respected by the post-colonial states, because to do otherwise would have threatened the entire continent with boundary disputes and instability. The result, however, was that African states did not correspond with nations. The single most unifying experience for the peoples of such states was frequently the struggle for independence from colonial rule. Once their colonial rulers were gone, such states faced the problems of nation-building, which meant motivating their citizens to feel a sense of commitment to the state rather than simply to their own people within the state.

---

8. I refer to Ferguson, *The State under Siege: Political Disintegration in the Post–Cold War Era* (in press) and Young, *The Rising Tide of Cultural Pluralism: The Nation-State at Bay?* (1993).

As we saw in Chapter 1, African leaders went to great lengths to denounce "tribalism," by which they meant a commitment to one's own people rather than to the state. They have often blamed the weakness of African states on the as yet unextinguished tribalism of their inhabitants. It has indeed proved difficult in Africa to secure the kind of commitment to the state that leaders desire, but this is not entirely due to the ethnic sentiments of their followers. In most parts of the continent, leaders have competed to control the state and to appropriate the spoils of government. They have played ethnic politics in order to accomplish this objective and, if successful, they have tended to recruit and reward their followers along ethnic lines. The state has thus become a prize for which ethnic groups, or in some cases cliques deriving from ethnic groups, compete. Either way, the potential for ethnic conflict has been considerable and the likelihood of instilling attachment to the state in the hearts of the citizenry correspondingly minimized.

In addition, post-colonial states are now forced to grapple with a new economic order that is disconcerting rich countries and leaving poorer countries devastatingly marginalized. A capitalism that emphasizes unfettered markets and free trade seems to dominate international dealings and threatens to impoverish the poorer nations that are marginal players (if they are players at all) in the global system. Furthermore, it is a different kind of capitalism from the one that was operating until the middle of the twentieth century. The old industries that built up the economic power of countries like Britain and the United States are less and less important. The countries that aspire to economic leadership in the future are looking to new industries such as microelectronics, the new materials-science industries, biotechnology, telecommunications, civilian aircraft manufacturing, robots with machine tools, and computers with software (Thurow 1992: 145). Moreover, the way these and other industries will be, indeed are already being, organized has been revolutionized and internationalized by the new technologies in computers and communications. In the emerging global marketplace, the state appears to be increasingly powerless to control its own economic destiny.[9] Meanwhile, ordinary people often come to feel that they are the victims of institutions and employers that do not care about their interests and

---

9. It was argued in *The Economist* (October 7–13, 1995) that the state had never possessed the powers of control over its economy that are commonly attributed to it. If true, this merely emphasizes the point I am making, namely that ordinary people are perturbed that things seem to be out of control and those in charge at the national level have no remedy for the situation.

could easily relocate their enterprises (and their jobs) in some foreign country.

Even the industrially most advanced countries—those on the northern side of the North–South divide that is now so much discussed—are not immune to such feelings of malaise. In the United States, voter anger and alienation has risen dramatically as the economy was restructured and many people have lost income, if not their jobs. In Western Europe, high levels of unemployment and concern that social benefits may not be maintained have made voters wary of, if not hostile toward, those wishing to immigrate into their countries. The economies of Russia and the former Soviet bloc countries are struggling. The effects on the relatively impoverished South are even more devastating, coming as they do at a time when the South (consisting of Africa and much of Asia and Latin America) is accusing the North of consuming more than its fair share of the world's resources, of rigging international trade to suit itself, and of being largely unwilling to help the countries of the South to escape from their poverty.

These economic changes have been accompanied by another phenomenon, the cumulative effect of which is beginning to be felt in international politics, namely population migrations. These are of two kinds—political refugees and migrants seeking a better future for themselves and their families. Sometimes, as with people leaving the former Yugoslavia and seeking to enter countries in Western Europe, or people leaving the war-torn countries of Central America and seeking asylum in the United States, it is hard to determine which category they fall into.[10] Such migrations have, in any case, reached massive proportions. Large numbers of people are moving from the South to the North—from Mexico and Latin America to the United States; from Asia to Canada to the United States and Western Europe; from North Africa, Turkey, and the Balkans to Western Europe, to name only the major currents. It is estimated that well over 200 million people are now living in countries to which they have emigrated. In addition to these, there are millions of refugees, forced out of their homes by local wars, taken in; when they are taken in, it is by reluctant host countries, and they obliged, as often as not, to live off international assistance. This is the economic and demographic back-

---

10. Such determinations are often highly political. At the height of the civil wars in Guatemala and El Salvador, the U.S. Immigration Service was instructed to treat refugees from those countries, where possible, as economic migrants and to refuse them entry, while migrants from Cuba were automatically granted refugee status.

ground against which the political changes of our new era have to be understood. These are, in effect, some of the important stress factors that contribute to the social climate of uncertainty where ethnic appeals can get a hearing.

My conclusions to this point are that ethnicity does not of itself promote conflict and undermine the state. It does, on the other hand, constitute a potentially volatile reservoir of divisiveness that can be activated with devastating results. How then is it possible to avoid situations in which the unscrupulous can kindle ethnic hatreds? Suppressing ethnic sentiments does not work. On the contrary, it merely focuses them until such time as they can be expressed, often in an especially virulent form. Ignoring them in the hope that they will weaken and disappear in the course of modernization, which has been the preferred solution in the west, does not work either. It follows, therefore, that the best policy is to seek to accommodate ethnicity somehow.

This is essentially the argument of Donald Horowitz's book *Ethnic Groups in Conflict* (1985), in which he analyzes situations where people have been unable to prevent the eruption of ethnic conflict, and those rarer polities where people have found ways to defuse it. One of the principal points that Horowitz makes is that countries that contain ethnic groups that are potentially in conflict must devise political systems where it is advantageous for politicians to appeal across ethnic lines. Otherwise, elections run the risk of being little more than censuses and are likely to have the effect of pitting the representatives of rival ethnic blocks against each other.

The Indonesian solution discussed in Chapter 2 makes a virtue out of ethnic diversity and tries to ensure that it does not blaze up into ethnic conflict by maintaining the authoritarian control of the government over the entire society. It bears certain similarities to the Stalinist system in the former Soviet Union. There, too, ethnic groups were formally recognized and the expression of their ethnicity was encouraged, but strict control over the whole society was maintained from Moscow. There are, of course, many differences between the two systems as well, but the most important major difference is that the Indonesians have been careful not to define the regions of their country in ethnic terms. It may be, for example, that Java is largely inhabited by Javanese, but it is not formally designated as a territory belonging to Javanese. The distinction may not seem to make much practical difference but it is of vital importance, for, as we have seen, the ethnic definition of the state is at the heart of nationalism.

This might seem to call the "Spanish solution," discussed in Chapter 2, into question. After all, Spain has adopted a federal system that devolves considerable authority to its provinces, at least two of which are defined ethnically—one for the Basques and one for the

Catalans[11]—but such a federal solution has built-in safeguards precisely because it is within the federation. The state is still Spain and Spanish authorities can see to it that the rights of minorities within the provinces are protected.

The real problem with such a system is how to prevent it from being used by ethnic entrepreneurs who seek to kindle nationalist and secessionist feelings, along the lines of what happened in the former Yugoslavia. Such people have, as we saw, already been active in the Basque country, but their local support diminished once a degree of autonomy was granted to the Basques. This confirms the idea that the best protection against those who seek to kindle ethnic hatred is to defuse nationalist sentiments by permitting the expression of ethnicity within the institutional arrangements of the state. This cannot be done in just any state. Nationalist divisiveness and ethnic conflict do not evaporate, for example, if a dictatorship is suddenly removed. They are more likely to be defused in a democratic state with a strong civil society.

Civil society is a term used to refer to those formal and informal ways of coming together and communicating with each other that people themselves generate. It is those voluntaristic aspects of society that lie between the givens of the family and the laws and institutions emanating from the state. It has been argued that people are less likely to heed the siren song of ethnic extremists if they live in a stable, democratic society in which they have confidence and in which they actively participate. The weakness or virtual absence of civil society was clearly one of the important contributory factors to the collapse of the Soviet Union and the break-up of Yugoslavia. The problem is that it is easier to enumerate the benefits of a strong civil society than it is to construct it, just as it is easier to understand the solidary virtues of small, traditional New England towns than it is to transplant those virtues to the alienated ghettoes of big cities.

If liberal, participatory democracy is suggested as the antidote to ethnic conflict, this also presents problems. In the first place, such democracies have not proved immune to ethnic appeals, as the growing strength of right-wing parties running on xenophobic platforms in western Europe has shown. Presumably the democratic solution requires democracies that are peculiarly stable, with a robustness to their civil societies that is not found everywhere. In the second place, most modern liberal democracies prefer, on both theoretical and practical grounds, not to accommodate ethnicity but to

---

11. It is also the ethnic definition of the province of Quebec that has proved to be such a destabilizing factor in Canada.

try to phase it out. Yet this is exactly what nationalists, even those who would be satisfied with local autonomy short of secession, fight against.

TRIBALISM AS MARGINALITY AND METAPHOR

Tribalism is a term that is almost always used pejoratively. I have already discussed the "tribalism" imputed to marginal or indigenous peoples and the "tribalism" so much criticized by African leaders. Here, I shall also discuss the "tribalism" that is thought by many to be undermining modern industrial states. Of course, the principal criticism leveled against tribalisms of all sorts is that they pose a threat to the state. The tribalism of indigenous peoples is thought to do this because such peoples are socially and often geographically marginal to the countries in which they live, and are regularly accused of wishing to secede, whether they actually wish to. They are also regularly accused of "standing in the way of development," though we saw in Chapter 1 that this accusation tells us more about the developers and their attitudes than it does about any real obstacles that indigenous peoples actually pose. But there is another sense in which the indigenous demand for cultural survival does pose a problem for the state. If, as I have just argued, most liberal democracies prefer in the long run to phase out ethnicity rather than to accommodate it, then the demand for indigenous rights is incompatible with this program.

The spokespeople for many indigenous groups in the United States, for example, argue that their peoples constitute nations who may have suffered the effects of the overwhelming power of the state in past years but whose sovereignty was never relinquished. Clearly, the idea that the American state should or does contain a large number of sovereign nations in its midst poses legal and constitutional problems that are not easy to resolve. But even a lesser formulation, as put forward in the Draft Declaration of Indigenous Rights at the United Nations, would, if accepted, change the administrative structure and current *modus operandi* of most states.

Indigenous peoples demand the protection of their own forms of governance, which poses the problem of how these are to be related to the form of governance that pertains in the country at large. They demand the protection of their traditional economic activities and their relation to the land, even though their traditional economic activities are often threatened by powerful interests and their lands (and their use of them) are a bone of contention between themselves and their nonindigenous neighbors. A government that accedes to these requests will have to change its way of operating in indigenous areas and, above all, may have to coerce its nonindigenous citizens to comply. This is not impossible, but it is often difficult, and governments are frequently reluctant to take the necessary steps to enforce such guarantees, as the Yanomami case discussed in Chapter 2 so clearly showed.

One kind of solution to this problem has recently been adopted by Canada, which has established the indigenous province of Nunavut in its far north. This area, as large as Alaska and Texas combined, is henceforward to be controlled by the Inuit.[12] The Inuit are giving up the title they claimed to even larger tracts of land and water in exchange for legally recognized ownership of a portion of the land over which they traditionally roamed and that they considered theirs. They will receive rights to minerals, gas, and oil on about 1 percent of the land, which has led some critics to argue that the Canadian government gave up little and in return received the recognized extinction of all aboriginal rights. The Inuit and their negotiators do not see it that way. Their population is small—there are about 22,000 people living in Nunavut, of whom 17,000 are Inuit. The ability of such small populations to defend their own rights against modern states is always questionable and the Inuit feel that their agreement with Canada has resolved a disputed issue involving adversaries much stronger than they are in a way that is good for them.

It is also worth noting that the creation of Nunavut for the Inuit is a *sui generis* solution that is not being applied elsewhere in Canada. The Dene Indians of the far north have been demanding a similar territorial settlement, but so far unsuccessfully. Meanwhile, there has been no interest on the part of Canadian provincial authorities in guaranteeing autonomous regions to other ethnic groups within their borders. This is especially ironic in the province of Quebec, which is demanding that Canada recognize francophone Quebecers as a distinct society, with its own right to autonomy and self-government, but simultaneously refusing to concede the same rights to the indigenous peoples who are the original inhabitants of Quebec.

The Canadian agreement with the Inuit is not (or at least not yet) a model for some kind of ethnic federalism in Canada. In Colombia, however, a new constitution adopted in 1991 does intend to be just that. It divides the country into territorial entities that elect their own local authorities and run their own affairs. Some of these districts will

---

12. *Inuit* is the self-designation of the people more commonly known as *Eskimo*. They reject the name *Eskimo* because it was a derogatory word applied to them by outsiders.

be officially indigenous ones run by their indigenous inhabitants, and non-Indians resident there will presumably have to submit to indigenous territorial authorities and obey indigenous laws. Some of these indigenous districts are also comparatively large because they are in the remote and thinly populated areas of the Amazon basin and the country's eastern plains. In this way, huge areas of Colombia appear to have been given over to indigenous local control. Nobody yet knows how or if these new arrangements will work because the state in Colombia has been weakened and local administrations disorganized by drug wars and armed insurrections. Yet, aside from their uncertain implementation, these new rules do contemplate a virtually revolutionary change, for they attempt to incorporate ethnic self-determination into the normal administrative apparatus of the state.

The difficulty of accommodating the rights of indigenous (or "tribal") peoples is only one aspect of the challenge posed by tribalism to the state, and not its most salient one. Usually when we hear criticisms of tribalism in the modern world, this refers to what I call *metaphorical tribalism*, or the tendency of people to band together with others of their own kind, rather than live up to their obligations—and indeed their potential—as citizens in the broadest sense, citizens, that is, of the state.

An eloquent argument to this effect was put forward by Peter Riesenberg in *Citizenship in the Western Tradition* (1992). There he argued that tribalism, with its clannishness and narrowing of horizons, is being revived in modern societies at every political level. This leads to conflict between groups within the state that no longer feel moral obligations to each other. Moreover, as this sense of moral obligation weakens, there is an increasing tendency to try to resolve problems by force rather than through discussion. In addition, there is a spreading belief that those who have suffered (or believe they have suffered) in the past are now justified in imposing suffering on others in return.

Riesenberg is, in effect, regretting the inability of western societies to achieve the enlightenment ideal of the state and blaming this inability on the tribalism of their citizens. It is this tribalism that supposedly leads to violence and undermines the civic culture of the state. Note, however, his telling comment that tribalism is all too frequently accompanied by the idea that people who have suffered in the past are entitled to impose suffering in the future on those who were responsible. In other words, the states he writes of have been societies where suffering was imposed. This has much to do with the "tribalism" of those who band together to protect themselves. The point is that the state and the groups within it are not distinct and static entities. They are entities that are constantly changing and interacting, to the extent of helping to define each other. If, therefore, suffering has been imposed in the past, the question then becomes how to break out of this vicious cycle of hurting and being hurt in order to persuade people to give their loyalty to the state instead of to subgroups that are arrayed against each other within the state.

There are two fundamental issues here. First, metaphorical tribalism is thought to undermine the civic culture on which the unitary state depends. Second, this is thought to lead to violence and conflict. Ethnic conflict is a great and legitimate fear, but it is important to see it, and indeed all violence in the modern world, in context. Violence in our time is not especially associated with ethnic divisions that undermine the state. That kind of violence obviously does take place, but violence is of many kinds. It is, for example, often visited by the state on its citizens. Nazi Germany, the Soviet Union, and Pol Pot's Cambodia are only the most glaring examples. It might be objected that the states just mentioned were hardly liberal democracies, and that metaphorical tribalism is criticized for being especially prone to undermining liberal democracies and to creating conflict within them. Yet the United States, for example, qualifies as a liberal democracy, but it also has an extraordinarily high level of interpersonal violence in comparison with other developed countries, and this violence is not particularly linked to tribalism. On the other hand, Canada, whose ethnic divisiveness is often held up as an example of what the United States should avoid, has a much lower level of interpersonal violence.

We tend, in effect, to idealize the peace and social order maintained by the unitary state and to exaggerate the threat posed to this vision by permitting cultural distinctiveness or local autonomy to ethnic groups within it. Still, even if this threat is often exaggerated, ethnic divisiveness is still a legitimate concern and it was this concern that Arthur Schlesinger Jr. addressed in his book *The Disuniting of America* (1992). Schlesinger argued that American minorities, who would once have been anxious to acquire the mainstream culture of the United States, are now tending more and more to insist on their distinctiveness and that they are being encouraged in this by the proponents of multiculturalism. It was therefore the multiculturalists[13] who drew his fire. They have argued that American education ought to be less Eurocentric and ought to teach and celebrate the diverse traditions of the various peoples that are represented in the American population.

---

13. With whom Schlesinger has done battle on curriculum committees, such as the one to revise the way social studies are taught in the public schools of New York state.

Schlesinger admitted that the way America and its culture had traditionally been presented in classrooms throughout the United States had reflected the traditions of only part of the country's population, excluding others and making them feel like second-class citizens. He argued, though, that the cure offered by the multiculturalists for this state of affairs was worse than the disease. He especially criticized the tendentious rewriting of history in order to produce curricula that made minorities feel good, the denial of any merit to western civilization, the insistence on foolish standards of political correctness, and the adoption of an anything-goes relativism. In conclusion, he argued that the United States should combat multiculturalism, virtually in defense of its own sanity, and certainly in defense of its own integrity and commitment to the search for truth. It should insist instead on its own common culture, properly taught to all its citizens through a curriculum suitably modified to be less exclusionary than before.

Schlesinger's critique of the absurdities of multiculturalism is convincing. Historical knowledge is inevitably interpretative and incorporates the point of view of the person who gathers it, but it does need to be gathered in as open-minded and critical a spirit as possible, and the best antidote to tendentious history is the professional scruples of the historians who judge it. It is dishonest and ultimately demoralizing, as George Orwell showed so vividly in his book about totalitarianism entitled *1984*, to teach distorted history, even if the intention is to improve the self-image of a minority within the nation. Similarly, a curriculum that ignores the backgrounds and histories of the ethnic minorities represented in the country is unsatisfactory, but so would a curriculum that ignored the European influence in the world and particularly on the United States. As for political correctness, many commentators besides Arthur Schlesinger have poked fun at or waxed indignant over the clumsy attempts of universities and other self-consciously multicultural institutions in American society to enforce standards of correct speech and behavior. Some of these standards are indeed ludicrous. It will not do, however, merely to criticize the standards and to offer no other remedy for the problems that the standards attempt to solve. Speech codes may be absurd, but what does one do about hate speech or racist graffiti or the desecration of other people's cemeteries and places of worship? Our society jealously guards its freedom of speech, but seems at a loss to know how to promote civilized communication and behavior when confronted with the kinds of racism and ethnic prejudice that can very well lead to conflict and killing.

Schlesinger does not address this question directly, but indirectly his book speaks to the issue. It is an eloquent appeal for the revival and strengthening of the civic culture that traditionally constituted the strength of America and the essence of Americanism. It was a culture shared by all Americans, regardless of creed or ethnic background, and inculcated in the schools and universities. It was this culture, he argues, that not only enabled America to live up to its motto "E Pluribus Unum" but also enabled the United States to avoid the kinds of ethnic conflicts that have bedeviled other parts of the world. It is this culture that he sees as being endangered by contemporary tribalism and multiculturalism. The balance is being tipped from the *unum* to the *pluribus* and this, in his view, poses a serious threat to America if it is allowed to continue.

I noted in Chapter 2, when contrasting "E Pluribus Unum" with Indonesia's motto of "Unity in Diversity," that the American idea focuses on the shedding or at least the weakening of ethnicity as immigrants become Americans, whereas the Indonesian idea accepts the indefinite continuation of diversity. The problem with Schlesinger's argument is that it pays little heed to those in America who do not wish to shed their ethnicity. Are they to be excluded from full participation in the wider society or is there a way in which they can legitimately maintain a distinctive ethnic culture and also be Americans?

In one sense, immigrants to the United States have always maintained their ethnicity if they so wished, but it was a private or semi-private matter. Though acceptably flaunted on occasions like Columbus Day or St. Patrick's Day, it was not given formal recognition in the public domain. Similarly, the defenders of American education point out that the monochrome, totally Eurocentric curricula so much criticized by the multiculturalists are a thing of the past. It seems that the United States is already groping for a way to recognize more of the diversity in its population without losing all sense of Americanism in the process.

Understandably, this does not please the extremists on either side. Extreme multiculturalists are dissatisfied with the progress made and conservatives think the whole process has gone too far and is undermining America's sense of itself. Conservatives tend to be particularly outraged by the relativism that they perceive as being taught in American classrooms. They claim that students are being taught that there are no objective standards by which one can judge another culture and, by extension, that there are no objective standards by which one can judge anything. This, in turn, induces in them an anything-goes relativism that renders them unable or unwilling to make serious judgments at all. This argument clearly connects with the conservative contention that the teaching of values is being seriously neglected in the classroom.

This is not the place to discuss what happens in American classrooms, but something needs to be said about relativism and especially about the relativism that is too often imputed to anthropologists. It is particularly anthropologists who stand accused of propounding an extreme relativism because it is thought that we are so anxious to communicate a sympathetic appreciation of other cultures, even those cultures whose practices might be considered reprehensible. The accusation is, however, unfounded, even technically absurd. If taken to its logical extreme, it would mean that if anthropologists determined that it was in the culture of Nazis to exterminate Jews, then they would have no reasonable grounds for criticizing the practice. I do not subscribe to such a view, nor does any other anthropologist I know. On the contrary, I espouse a serious relativism grounded in anthropological principles, which is very different from the anything-goes relativism of the conservative caricatures. It is a relativism that directly contradicts the old French aphorism that "To understand all is to forgive all." Like most aphorisms, this one feels like a truth, but in fact is just the opposite. It suggests that understanding involves a total identification with the views and actions one seeks to understand, otherwise it does not count as full understanding. But this is an absurd view of "understanding." I submit that it is quite possible to understand Nazis without sympathizing with them and that virtually all understanding of people and societies stops short of such total identification with them. The fundamental procedures of the serious relativism I defend here are methodological and they involve three stages: first, a temporary suspension of judgment on an alien culture and its customs; second, a presumption of tolerance for that culture and those customs; third, the formulation of judgments concerning the culture and its customs. These precepts are very hard to put into practice, for in our everyday lives we judge and prejudge so automatically that we come to do it without thinking and it takes much effort to put our prejudices (and sometimes the very categories of our own language) on hold. The point of these procedures is to try to suspend judgment until we have gained understanding—not in order to avoid judgment, but in order to make better informed judgments. It is an intellectual stance that takes the making of judgments very seriously and seeks constantly to revise and improve the judgments that one makes.

Multiculturalism at its best, or what I shall call serious multiculturalism, involves a strenuous effort to come to terms with the diversity of the world in which we live and with the country in which we live. Its purpose in the United States is not to make different peoples feel good, although that would be an added bonus if it did, but rather to be intellectually honest about the American heritage. Most of all, it is the active aspect of the tolerance and openness to other cultures that is necessary if people are to make multiethnic societies work anywhere.

That is why a discussion of ethnicity and the state leads logically into a discussion of education for, as I argued earlier, a state can only function as a multiethnic system if its citizens are educated in tolerance and its civil society is working reasonably well. That is why social theorists stress the need either for a basic consensus or for control at the national level in multiethnic societies.

Michael Walzer put it even more strongly when he wrote that "for the moment...pluralism in the strong sense—one state, many peoples— is possible only under tyrannical regimes" (1982: 6). Nevertheless, in the same paper he foresaw other possibilities, such as decentralization, devolution, and federalism as ways for ethnically plural or what he called "composite" states to survive; but he was not optimistic about their prospects, suggesting that it was not certain whether composite states could survive as federations, but unlikely that they could survive in any other way (1982: 4–5). Later on, he suggested that the state in multiethnic societies would have to defend collective as well as individual rights and, in effect, guarantee the circumstances under which ethnic groups can thrive (1982: 19).

The problem with such a guarantee is, as we have seen, that it involves the state in the business of protecting group rights rather than the individual rights that have been at the heart of enlightenment thinking about democracy and the social contract. It has to protect them in a particular way, not just procedurally, which is to say by ensuring that members of a group are treated as equitably as everybody else in the society. It must recognize that the distinctive beliefs and practices of ethnic groups have value, even though they are not shared by other groups within the society and may not be shared by the majority of the society.[14] It is one thing, however, to say that there is value in other cultural traditions and quite another to maintain or, worse still, be required to maintain that other traditions are admirable. A culture has value in its own right simply because it is the way of life of a distinct people, so that it must be respected if they are to be respected. It can be hoped but cannot be demanded, as it has been by some extreme multiculturalists, that respect will also include admiration for the culture and its products. Such a demand is especially contradictory if it is made by people who have already denied that there are grounds for making valid judgments about other cultures in the first place.[15]

If we cannot demand that the traditions of another culture be found admirable, can we at least demand that they not be found reprehensible? No, we cannot demand that either. The serious relativism

---

14. See Taylor 1994 for a discussion of the difference between procedural liberalism and the politics of difference.
15. For a discussion of this issue, see Gutmann (1994) and Taylor (1994).

that I defend here is based on a presumption of tolerance for other ways of life in order to understand them better. That is inevitably followed, especially in multiethnic societies, by judgments. A society that is striving earnestly to be open to different traditions among its citizenry may nevertheless find some traditions unacceptable. A minority in the United States would not be allowed, for example, to practice human sacrifice even if this were part of its religion; but what if traditionalists from the Indian subcontinent wanted to practise *suttee* (the custom of requiring widows to immolate themselves on their husbands' funeral pyres)? How about female circumcision, or sexism, or lack of due process in trials, or absence of a secret ballot in decision making? Clearly, there is a hierarchy of practices about which a society might be required to make judgments. It is relatively easy to reach decisions on the more extreme ones. Decisions on others will be much harder and will require the society at large to weigh the harm done by the practice against the harm done to the minority (and indeed to the multiethnic state itself) by denying that minority's tradition. The point is that cultural survival is an important right, and one that must be respected if multiethnic societies are to work at all, but it is not an absolute one.

Nor, as Habermas points out (1994), can the state guarantee the cultural survival of the minorities within it. The best it can do is to ensure that the rights of minorities are protected in such a way that they have a reasonable opportunity to ensure their own cultural continuity. In Chapter 1 I argued that the cultural survival of indigenous peoples depends on similar opportunities being made available to them. The cultural survival of all kinds of minorities, be they indigenous, localized, dispersed, or incipient nations, depends on the willingness and the ability of the state to act in an enabling fashion. This, in turn, requires that the state consider cultural distinctiveness within it to be legitimate and that it make administrative arrangements to accommodate it. The various ways of doing this are well known. It can be accomplished through some kind of devolution or decentralization of the powers of the state in some kind of federal system. Alternatively, in states with dispersed and self-conscious minorities, it can be accomplished through what I have called serious multiculturalism. Why then does it happen relatively infrequently— so rarely in fact that many reasonable people think that multiethnic states cannot function smoothly and peacefully?

The answer, I believe, lies in the complexity of the undertaking and the precarious stability of the desired result. Multiethnic states require immense social effort if they are to function well. They require more than a willingness to accommodate ethnicity. They depend on nationwide education in tolerance, on the control of hate speech, and on the presence of a strong civil society. Such processes are difficult to institutionalize and to sustain, particularly in the framework of a liberal democracy.

The control of hate speech and incitement to interethnic violence is particularly hard. An outright ban poses various kinds of problems: of definition (exactly what kinds of utterances or acts are to be banned and how?), of liberty (how can such a ban be reconciled with the democratic principle that people are free to speak their minds without fear of punishment?), and of execution (who is to enforce the ban, under what circumstances, and against whom?). In countries that do try to enforce such a ban, it is often used as a political weapon against minorities who complain about unjust treatment at the hands of the majority and are then indicted for incitement of interethnic hatred. Since genuine incitement rather than this spurious kind is the main ingredient in ethnic conflict, this poses a real dilemma.

If a society does make the effort to promote interethnic harmony and succeeds, it has no guarantee of living happily ever after. Rather, it achieves a balance—as precarious as all balances—between the rights of the individual and the rights of groups, between unity and diversity, between *pluribus* and *unum*. It is small wonder, then, that this happens so infrequently, but that is no reason to believe that it cannot happen at all. After all, it was not so long ago that it was generally thought that democracy was an equally precarious system that could not work very well. The skeptics had a point. Democracy is difficult to institutionalize, riven with inefficiencies and excesses, and all too vulnerable to the misuse of the freedoms that it prizes. Yet this does not deter us from trying to make it work, because we choose this form of organization on moral grounds. I suggest that the same is true for multiethnic states. Most states in the present are multiethnic and the tendency is for more and more states to become so in the future. Making such states work in a spirit of tolerance and serious multiculturalism is thus a moral imperative as well as a practical possibility. The alternatives are, as we have seen, exceedingly unpleasant to contemplate.

5

Different States, Different World

It is clear that ethnicity is not simply an innate propensity of human beings to bond with those like them and to fight with those unlike them. It is a potential that must be activated and cultivated. Therefore, in this book I have paid attention to the agents who call forth ethnic sentiment and the circumstances under which they do so. One might say that the creation and manipulation of ethnicity are the most important aspects to study if one wishes to understand the phenomenon.

It is also important to note that ethnicity does not automatically imply conflict. It is vitally important to study ethnic conflicts so that we may better understand the circumstances that produced them, and equally vital to study the circumstances under which ethnic groups do not enter into conflict with each other.

The entire discussion, even when it focused on the particular circumstances of indigenous peoples or nationalities within states, depended throughout on an understanding of the role of the state. I tried to indicate what was, at any given moment, the national agenda of the state in question, namely, what were the basic understandings and goals of the people in power and in terms of which they framed their policies.

The discussion started with a consideration of genocide, the ultimate breakdown in interethnic civility, and the one commonly used against indigenous peoples because they are, by definition, aliens. It ended, alas, with further consideration of genocide as the ultimate expression of created alienation between peoples in modern states. Indeed, the entire discussion of ethnicity and ethnic conflict is stalked by the specter of genocide. We all know that if ethnicity is allowed—or worse still, encouraged—to degenerate into ethnic conflict, then ethnic cleansing and genocide remain real possibilities, even in supposedly "modern" countries.

The United Nations realized this after the second world war. It was the horror inspired by the genocidal Nazi regime, coupled with a determination to create a new world order that would prevent a repetition of such atrocities, that led the newly formed world body to pass a resolution against the crime of genocide as early as 1946. Even at that time, the resolution was not easy to pass. There was considerable argument about the precise definition of genocide and which kinds of groups had to be massacred before the crime counted as genocide.[1]

The massacre of a group of people defined by their political views was, for example, struck out as constituting genocide. Similarly, the massacre of the *kulaks* (wealthier peasants) by Stalin's regime in the 1930s would not count either, although millions died. It could be counted as genocide under the original declaration only if it were argued that the *kulaks* were massacred because they were Ukrainians (as many of them were), but even that argument might not be sufficient if it were shown that Ukrainians were only some of those who were killed. The Soviet Union and its satellites did ratify the genocide convention in 1948, but with the reservation that they refused to be bound by the provision that the International Court of Justice should have jurisdiction in such cases. The United States refused to ratify the convention at that time. American ratification came only in 1989 and it was accompanied by a reservation similar to the Soviet one, namely that if the United States were involved in a case of genocide, it would only accept the jurisdiction of the International Court of Justice if it chose to do so.[2]

More disheartening even than the arguments about the definition of genocide is the fact that the existence of the United Nations Declaration, with all its signatories and ratifiers, together with the existence of the International Court of Justice, have neither been able to prevent the numerous genocides that have taken place since World War II nor to punish the perpetrators of them. The reasons for this are not hard to find. Genocide is invariably carried out by forces who control the region where people are massacred—in other words, by governments or others who act like governments. It can therefore only be prevented by forces external to the region who are both willing and able to re-

---

1. Much of my information on the legal and political arguments surrounding the definition of genocide is drawn from Lori Damrosch's "Genocide and Ethnic Conflict."
2. It was at about this time that Russia and the newly independent republics of the former Soviet Union dropped their formal objection to the jurisdiction of the International Court of Justice.

strain those who control it. This means that genocide can only be prevented by the action of an external power or by external powers acting in concert. Yet, the whole system of international order in the world is based on respect for national sovereignty, on the presumption that states should not interfere in the internal affairs of other states. It is extremely difficult to persuade powerful states to intervene in order to prevent genocide and equally difficult to gain the necessary consensus for an international force to carry out this task.

The genocide in Rwanda is a case in point. Many people, both inside and outside Rwanda, knew it was impending. Hutu were being openly incited over the radio to massacre the Tutsi (and moderate Hutu as well). Yet the regional international organization—the Organization of African Unity—did not intervene. Nor did the United Nations, which actually had "peacekeeping forces" in Rwanda during the massacre. These forces stood by and allowed it to happen because they had no orders and were not strong enough to intervene. Meanwhile, none of the great powers found that it was in their national interest to get involved.

A similar hesitancy marked the world's reactions to the conflict and its accompanying massacres in Bosnia. During the years of the killings, the United Nations sent troops to Bosnia, but defined their mission as humanitarian, which succeeded in endangering the soldiers, allowing the killings to continue, and raising the level of world cynicism, not only about the prevention of genocide but also about the very possibility of enforcing peace between warring parties.

Eventually, peacekeepers were sent to Bosnia, but this was done after the worst of the fighting and the ethnic cleansing had run its course. It is noteworthy that one of the provisions of the peace treaty that put an end to the fighting in Bosnia was that those indicted for war crimes committed during the hostilities should not be allowed to remain in power. A number of people have, in fact, been indicted for crimes committed in Bosnia and elsewhere in the former Yugoslavia, but they have not been removed from power. Milosevic in Serbia continued in power until his own people voted him out, and he is still trying to make a political comeback. Others under indictment have simply retired from the limelight. They face the possibility of being arrested and sent to stand trial before the International Court of Justice at The Hague, but the peacekeeping forces that occupy their home territories have shown little inclination to arrest them.

On the other hand, the government of Rwanda is determined to prosecute those responsible for the genocide in that country. It is, with the help of legal experts from other countries, attempting to assign greater and lesser responsibility to the hundreds and thousands of people accused of participating in the massacres. In this way, it hopes to develop legal procedures for publishing the most serious offenders in a court system that is understaffed and underfunded for such a mammoth task.

Rwanda is at least governed at present by the people who were victimized during the genocide, and this government has some of the perpetrators in prison awaiting trial. The apprehension and indictment other senior figures, who have fled the country, must depend, as it does in the former Yugoslavia, on the willingness and ability of the international community to make this a priority and to put pressure on those countries who might otherwise harbor the fugitives.

The cruel fact of the matter is that the most heinous crime of all—namely the massacre of a whole category of people simply because of who they are—can only be prevented or punished by international action, and international action is normally undermined by individual nations' calculations of their own interests. This faces us with a cruel dilemma, as Stanley Hoffmann pointed out when he wrote about the promotion of human rights in *Duties Beyond Borders* (1981: 139–40). Either the present system of nation-states has such a high degree of tolerance for violations of human rights, even for genocide, that one must hope for a new world order to remedy the situation; or one can simply accept the present state of affairs, genocide and all, avert one's eyes to the horrors that states commit within their own borders, and make sure that they treat each other with moderation in international affairs. Hoffmann noted that not even the blueprint for a workable new world order had yet been developed. On the other hand, the "realistic" policy of accepting things the way they are and trying to keep the peace internationally makes the very unrealistic assumption that the internal affairs of states, even their genocides, will not affect their external relations. So what can be done? Hoffmann suggests that we accept the realists' warning that the promotion of human rights (even the prevention of genocide) should not be the sole object of foreign policy, but not let this inhibit our efforts to create a better international order. Similarly, we should not allow the fact that the new order seems very far off to inhibit our efforts to get there. We should constantly seek out possibilities for progress in international affairs until such time as the world may be willing and able to act on its abhorrence of genocide.

There are some slight indications of progress in this direction. The world has repeatedly stood by while the Kurds of Turkey, Iran, and Iraq have been massacred, yet at the end of the Gulf War, when the defeated Saddam Hussein was nevertheless left in control of Iraq, he was deprived by the United Nations of control over the northern, Kurdish area of his country. The international community acted belatedly in Bosnia to stop the war and to set up a standing international court with jurisdiction over crimes such as genocide, something that had been contemplated in the aftermath of the second world war but allowed to languish until recently.

Such small straws in the winds of change are perhaps little consolation, but they do offer us hope that more effective efforts will be made in the new order of the post–cold war world to deal with the worst excesses of ethnic conflict. Meanwhile, the best way to avoid repeating the horrors of the present in the not too distant future is to better understand both the past and the present. That has been the purpose of this study. It is important, for example, to understand that human beings are not driven to conflict by primordial ethnic urges and further to understand not only that such conflicts are largely created, but also how they are created. It is important to know that indigenous peoples are neither subversive nor fated for extinction, so that we can learn to live and let them live. It is equally important to understand that states can be both peaceable and multiethnic, so that we can learn to make such systems work. It is most important of all that peoples as well as individual people should know, not only that it is desirable to get along with each other if they share a single state, but also that it has been and can be done.

References

Anderson, Benedict
   1983.   Imagined Communities: Reflections on the Origin and Spread
           of Nationalism. London: Verso.

Aragon, Lorraine V.
   1994.   "Multiculturalism: Some Lessons from Indonesia" In Cultural
           Survival Quarterly 18 (2 & 3): 72–76.

Aretxaga, Begoña
   1994.   "Ethnic Violence and the Making of Pluralist Spain." In Cultural
           Survival Quarterly 18 (2 & 3): 44–47.

Barfield, Thomas J.
   1994.   "Prospects for Plural Societies in Central Asia." In Cultural Sur-
           vival Quarterly 18 (2 & 3): 48–51.

Barth, Fredrik
   1969.   Ethnic Groups and Boundaries. Boston: Little Brown.

Berlin, Isaiah
   1979.   Against the Current: Essays in the History of Ideas. London:
           Hogarth.

Bodley, John H.
   1975.   Victims of Progress. Menlo Park, CA: Cummings Publishing
           Company.

Brown, Michael F. and Eduardo Fernández
   1991.   War of Shadows: The Struggle for Utopia on the Peruvian Ama-
           zon. Berkeley: University of California Press.

Cultural Survival
   1987.   Southeast Asian Tribal Groups and Ethnic Minorities: Prospects
           for the Eighties and Beyond. Cambridge, MA: Cultural Sur-
           vival.

Cultural Survival
   1994.   "Special Report: Why Chiapas?" In Cultural Survival Quarterly
           (Spring): 14–34.

Damrosch, Lori F.
           "Genocide and Ethnic Conflict." Presented at the Workshop on
           International Law and Ethnic Conflict, November 10–11, 1995.

De Waal, Alex
1994. "Genocide in Rwanda." Anthropology Today 10 (3): 1–2.

Denich, Bette
Forthcoming. "Superfluity and Schismogenesis in the Dismantling of Yugoslavia." In R. Brian Ferguson, ed., The State under Siege: Political Disintegration in the Post–Cold War Era.

Denitch, Bogdan
1994. Ethnic Nationalism: The Tragic Death of Yugoslavia. Minneapolis, MN: University of Minnesota Press.

Djilas, Aleksa
1991. The Contested Country: Yugoslav Unity and Communist Revolution, 1919–1953. Cambridge, MA: Harvard University Press.

Enloe, Cynthia
1973. Ethnic Conflict and Political Development. Boston: Little, Brown and Company.

Fein, Helen, ed.
1994. "The Prevention of Genocide: Rwanda and Yugoslavia Reconsidered," A Working Paper of the Institute for the Study of Genocide.

Ferguson, R. Brian, ed.
In press. The State under Siege: Political Disintegration in the Post–Cold War Era.

Fisher, William F., ed.
1995. Toward Sustainable Development?: Struggling Over India's Narmada River. Armonk, NY: M.E. Sharpe.

Fondahl, Gail A., ed.
1992. "After the Breakup: Roots of Soviet Dis-Union." Cultural Survival Quarterly 16 (1), Winter.

Galeano, Eduardo
1985. Memory of Fire: I. Genesis, trans. Cedric Belfrage. New York: Pantheon Books.

Gellner, Ernest
1983. Nations and Nationalism. Ithaca: Cornell University Press.

Gilmour, David
1985. The Transformation of Spain: From Franco to the Constitutional Monarchy. London: Quartet Books.

Glenny, Misha
1992. The Fall of Yugoslavia: The Third Balkan War. London: Penguin Books.

Gutmann, Amy, ed.
1994. Multiculturalism: Examining the Politics of Recognition. Princeton: Princeton University Press.

Habermas, Jürgen
1994. "Struggles for Recognition in the Democratic Constitutional State." In A. Gutmann, ed., Multiculturalism: Examining the Politics of Recognition. Princeton: Princeton University Press: 107–148.

Hanke, Lewis
1959. Aristotle and the American Indians: A Study in Race Prejudice in the Modern World. Bloomington, IN: Indiana University Press.

Hayden, Robert
1995. "Serbian and Croatian Nationalism and the Wars in Yugoslavia." In Cultural Survival Quarterly 19 (2): 25–28.

Heberer, Thomas
1989. China and Its National Minorities. New York: M.E. Sharpe.

Hobsbawm, E. J.
1990. Nations and Nationalism Since 1780: Programme, Myth and Reality. Cambridge: Cambridge University Press.

Hobsbawm, Eric
1993. "The New Threat to History." In The New York Review of Books XI (21): 62–64.

Hodgkin, Thomas
1962. African Political Parties. Harmondsworth, UK: Penguin.

Hoffmann, Stanley
1981. Duties Beyond Borders: On the Limits and Possibilities of Ethical International Politics. Syracuse: Syracuse University Press.

Horowitz, Donald L.
1985. Ethnic Groups in Conflict. Berkeley: University of California Press.

Horowitz, Michael
1979. The Sociology of Pastoralism and African Livestock Projects. Washington, DC: USAID/GPO.

Kaapcke, Gretchen
1992. "Indigenous Identity Transition in Russia." In Cultural Survival Quarterly 18 (2 & 3): 62–68.

Kipp, Rita Smith
1993. Dissociated Identities: Ethnicity, Religion and Class in an Indonesian Society. Ann Arbor: University of Michigan Press.

Leitenberg, Milton
1994. "US and UN Actions Escalate Genocide and Increase Costs in Rwanda," in Fein, ed., "The Prevention of Genocide: Rwanda and Yugoslavia Reconsidered," A Working Paper of the Institute for the Study of Genocide, 33–43.

Lemarchand, René
  1994.   "The Apocalypse in Rwanda." In Cultural Survival Quarterly
          18 (2 & 3): 29–33.

Lijphart, Arend
  1977.   "Political Theories and the Explanation of Ethnic Conflict in the
          Western World." In Milton J. Esman, ed., Ethnic Conflict in the
          Western World. Ithaca: Cornell University Press.

Mackerras, Colin
  1994.   China's Minorities: Integration and Modernization in the Twen-
          tieth Century. Oxford: Oxford University Press.

Maybury-Lewis, David
  1992.   Millennium: Tribal Wisdom and the Modern World. New York:
          Viking.

Merivale, Herman
  1842.   Lectures on Colonialism and the Colonies, vol. 2. London:
          Longman, Orine, Brown, Green, and Longmans.

Mill, John Stuart
  1861/1951.   Considerations on Representative Government. New
          York: E. P. Dutton.

Mirante, Edith T.
  1987.   "Ethnic Minorities of the Burma Frontiers and Their Resistance
          Groups." In Cultural Survival, Southeast Asian Tribal Groups
          and Ethnic Minorities: Prospects for the Eighties and Beyond.
          Cambridge, MA: Cultural Survival.

Nadirov, Nadir
  1992.   "Population Transfer: A Scattered People." In Cultural Survival
          Quarterly 16 (1): 38–40.

Nash, Manning
  1989.   The Cauldron of Ethnicity in the Modern World. Chicago: Uni-
          versity of Chicago Press.

Newbury, Catharine
  1988.   The Cohesion of Oppression: Clientship and Ethnicity in
          Rwanda 1860–1960. New York: Columbia University Press.

Payin, Emil
  1992a. "Population Transfer: Crimean Tatars Return Home." In Cul-
          tural Survival Quarterly 16 (1): 33–35.

Payin, Emil
  1992b. "Population Transfer: Tragedy of the Meskhetian Turks." In
          Cultural Survival Quarterly 16 (1): 36–37.

Ramos, Alcida Rita
  1995.   Sanumá Memories: Yanomami Ethnography in Times of Crisis.
          Madison, WI: University of Wisconsin Press.

Riesenberg, Peter N.
  1992.   Citizenship in the Western Tradition: Plato to Aristotle. Chapel
          Hill: University of North Carolina Press.

Roosevelt, Theodore
  1889.   The Winning of the West: From the Alleghenies to the Missis-
          sippi, 1769–1776, vol. I. New York: G. P. Putnam's Sons.

Schlesinger, Arthur M. Jr.
  1992.   The Disuniting of America: Reflections on a Multicultural Soci-
          ety. New York: W. W. Norton & Co.

Schoeberlein-Engel, John S.
  In press. "Toppling the Balance: The Creation of Inter-Ethnic War in
          Tajikistan."

Serres Güiraldes, Alfredo M.
  1979.   La Estrategia de General Roca. Buenos Aires: Pleamar.

Szpörluk, Roman
  1990.   "The Imperial Legacy and the Soviet Nationalities Problem." In
          Lubomyr Hajda and Mark Beissinger, eds., The Nationalities
          Factor in Soviet Politics and Society. Boulder, CO: Westview
          Press: 1–23.

Taussig, Michael
  1986.   Shamanism, Colonialism, and the Wild Man: A Study in Terror
          and Healing. Chicago: University of Chicago Press.

Taylor, Charles
  1994.   "The Politics of Recognition" In A. Gutmann, ed., Multicultur-
          alism: Examining the Politics of Recognition. Princeton: Prince-
          ton University Press: 25–73.

Thurow, Lester
  1992.   Head to Head: The Coming Economic Battle Among Japan,
          Europe and America. New York: William Morrow and Company.

Tishkov, Valery
  1994.   "Perspectives on Ethnic Accord in Post-Soviet Space." In Cul-
          tural Survival Quarterly 18 (2 & 3): 52–57.

Touré, Sekou
  1959.   Towards Full Re-Africanization. Paris: Présence Africaine.

Vincent, Joan
  1974.   "The Structuring of Ethnicity." In Human Organization 33:
          375–379.

von Fürer-Haimendorf, Christoph
1982. Tribes of India: The Struggle for Survival. Berkeley: University of California Press.

Walzer, Michael
1982. "Pluralism in Political Perspective." In M. Walzer, ed., The Politics of Ethnicity. Cambridge: Belknap Press of Harvard University Press: 1–28.

Wixman, Ronald and Don Dumond
1992. "A People Dwindling Under Centralized Rule." In Cultural Survival Quarterly 16 (1): 57–60.

Yamskov, Anatoly N.
1994. "The 'New Minorities' in Post-Soviet States." In Cultural Survival Quarterly 18 (2 & 3): 58–61.

Young, Crawford, ed.
1993. The Rising Tide of Cultural Pluralism: The Nation-State at Bay? Madison, WI: University of Wisconsin Press.

Index

marginalized, 45
and the need to be "civilized," 25
numbers of, 8–10
population loss, 8–10
secession not normally advocated
   by, 32, 46, 135
undermining the state, 25, 31–32, 46
wishing to secede from state, 32, 46
Indonesia, 9, 11, 37–42, 68–73,
   115, 119
transmigration, 72
Irian Jaya (Indonesia), 39, 72
Ituri rainforest, 9
Japan, 8, 10, 35, 41
Java, 69, 119
Jewish Autonomous Territory in
   former Soviet Union, 54–55
Juárez, Benito, 13

Kachin, 41
Kalahari desert, 9
Karens, 40
Kassam, Aneesa, 28
Kazakhstan, 61
Kenya, 29, 43, 87
Kirghizstan, 61–62
Kurds
   in former Soviet Union, 54
   in Turkey, Iran, and Iraq, 134

Laos, 40
Lapps (Sami), 9
Las Casas, Bartolome de, 11
League of Nations, 111
Lenin, V. I., 52
Lijphart, Arend, 112–113

Machiavelli, Niccoló, 105
Madison, James, 106
Maoris, 6, 8, 9
Marcos, Subcommander, 16–17
Malaysia, 37
Mao Zedong, 65–66, 77
Mariátegui, José, 24, 32
Maya Indians, 2, 15–17
Mexico, 8–9, 13–17, 24–25
   pluriethnic, 14
   Zapatista rebellion, 14–17
Mill, John Stuart, 108
Milosevic, Slobodan, 95–96, 98, 133
Mobutu, Sese Seko, 86
Mongols, 26, 63, 67
Montagnards (Vietnam), 40
Montaigne, Michel, 11
Multiculturalism
   attacked, 124–125
   balance, 130
   defended, 126, 127–128

education in tolerance for, 127, 129
   peaceful, 135
Museveni, Yoweri, 84
Myanmar (see Burma)

NAFTA (North American Free Trade
   Agreement), 16–17
Naga, 33
   independence denied, 35
Nation, 108
   as distinct from state, 108–109, 121
Nationalism, 108, 111
   Chinese concept of, 110
   Nation-states, 110
National minorities, 45 (see also Ethnic
   minorities)
New Zealand, 6, 8, 9
Nigeria, 43
Nkruma, Kwame, 43
Nomads, 26–29
North-South Divide, 117–118
Norway, 9

Pacific Islands, 8, 9
Papuans, 39, 72
Peru, 20
   Indigenismo in, 24, 32
Philippines, 8, 9, 38
Population migrations, 118
Portugal, 2–3
PRI (Mexican Institutional
   Revolutionary Party), 15, 17
Primordial conflicts (see Tribal conflicts)
Putumayo atrocities, 4, 5, 10
Pygmies (Efe), 9, 42

Quebec, 48, 122

Ramos, Alcida, 21–23
Relativism, 126–127, 128–129
Riesenberg, Peter, 123
Roca, General Julio, 3
Rondon, Candido Mariano
   da Silva, 18
Roosevelt, Theodore, 3, 12, 18
Rousseau, Jean-Jacques, 11, 106
Russia, 9
Rwanda, 81–88, 115, 133, 134

Salinas de Gortari, 15–17
Sardar Sarovar Dam, 35
Scandinavia, 8
Scheduled tribes (India), 33, 36–37
Schlesinger Jr., Arthur, 124
Self-determination, 46
   acquired bad name, 112
   threat to Ottoman and European
      empires, 91
Sepúlveda, Juan de, 11, 25